THE AMERICAN SIGN LANGUAGE PHRASE BOOK

LOU FANT

ILLUSTRATIONS BY BETTY G. MILLER

CONTEMPORARY BOOKS

A TRIBUNE COMPANY

Library of Congress Cataloging-in-Publication Data

Fant, Louie J.
    The American sign language phrase book / Lou Fant ; illustrations
by Betty G. Miller.
        p.   cm.
    Includes index.
    ISBN 0-8092-3500-5 (paper)
    1. American sign language—Dictionaries.   I. Miller, Betty G.
II. Title.
HV2475.F36   1994
419—dc20   94-18884
                                                                         CIP

Published by Contemporary Books
An imprint of NTC/Contemporary Publishing Company
Two Prudential Plaza, Chicago, Illinois 60601-6790
Manufactured in the United States of America
International Standard Book Number: 0-8092-3500-5
10   9   8   7   6

Contents

PREFACE TO THE REVISED EDITION   **vi**

1. HOW TO USE THIS BOOK   **1**

2. A GUIDE TO AMERICAN SIGN LANGUAGE   **17**

3. EVERYDAY EXPRESSIONS   **74**

Hello • Good morning • Good afternoon • Good night • How are you? • How have you been? • I'm glad to see you • Where is the rest room? • See you later • Good-bye • Close/open the door/window • I feel fine/sick/tired/lousy/all right/wonderful • Do you have a car? • I haven't seen you for a long time • Thank you • Please • Pardon me • Do you like to watch T.V.? • Do you want to go to the movies? • What's your phone number? • Do you have a TTY? • May I go with you? • Have a seat, please • What time is it? • I have to go home • Where are you going? • I'm sorry

4. SIGNING AND DEAFNESS   **89**

I'm learning sign language • Sign slowly, please • Please repeat • I can't fingerspell well • I can fingerspell but I can't read it well • You sign fast • I don't understand • Would you write it, please? • How do you sign _____? • There's no sign for that; you have to fingerspell it • What does _____ mean? • Are you deaf/hearing/hard-of-hearing? • Do you use a hearing aid? • Can you read lips? • I speak a little • How did you lose your hearing? • How old were you when you became deaf? • I was born deaf • Are your parents deaf? • I want to visit a club for deaf people • I enjoy watching T.V. with captions • I saw a captioned film last night • Did you go to a residential school for deaf children? • I went to a school for hearing children • Gallaudet College was the first college for deaf people • Many deaf students enter hearing colleges • Gallaudet College is in Washington, D.C. • Blind people read braille; deaf people do not

5. GETTING ACQUAINTED   **106**

What is your name? • My name is _____ • I'm happy to meet you • Where do you live? • Where are you from? • Where were you born? • May I introduce my wife/husband/son/daughter/friend? • Where do you work? • What kind of work do you do? • I'm a doctor • Do you go to school? • Are you married? • I'm single/divorced/widowed • Do you have any children? • How many children do you have? • How old are you? • Do you mind if I smoke? • It's all right • Smoking is not allowed • Do you have a light? • Additional vocabulary words

6. HEALTH   **121**

How do you feel? • Do you feel all right? • I don't feel well • Where does it hurt? • My stomach is upset • I have a cold • My nose is runny • My head aches • I have a toothache/stomachache • I need a dentist/doctor • Do you have any aspirin? • I've run out of medicine • I have to buy some medicine • I have to take pills • You need to have an x-ray • It's time to take your temperature • You have to have a shot • I feel better now • I was in bed for two weeks • Were any bones broken? • You lost a lot of blood • They have to draw some blood • Have you ever had a tooth pulled? • I had a physical last week • My husband had an operation • My wife is in the hospital • My father passed away last month • Call the ambulance • I have an appointment at 2:30 • Where's my toothbrush? • I want to brush my teeth • I already took a bath/shower • Wash your hands/face • I haven't shaved yet • May I borrow your hair dryer? • Brush your hair • I lost my comb • Do you have hospitalization insurance?

7. WEATHER   **142**

It's beautiful today • The sun is hot • I enjoy sitting in the sun • It was cold this morning • It will freeze tonight • Maybe it will snow tomorrow • There was thunder and lightning last night • It rained yesterday • Do you have a raincoat? • I lost my umbrella • Where are your galoshes/rubbers? • It's windy today • Yesterday evening at sunset, the clouds were beautiful • I hope it clears up this afternoon • I like spring/summer/autumn/winter best • You have to use chains to drive in the mountains in winter • I'm afraid of tornados • What's the temperature? • Has the snow melted? • There was a flood last year • The temperature is below zero • Have you ever been in an earthquake?

8. FAMILY   **154**

Your father is nice looking • You look like your mother • My brother is younger than I • My sister speaks several languages fluently • His son wants to be an astronaut • Her daughter works here • My uncle is a farmer • My aunt lives in town • Your nephew game me a book • My cousin is a pilot • Who is that man? • Did you see the woman? The baby is cute • The girl told the boy that she loves him • Father told the little boy to play outside • The girl's doll is broken • How many children are coming? Our family is large/small • We had a family reunion last summer • We met at Grandfather's farm

9. SCHOOL   **170**

Do you go to school? • I go to college • I'm majoring in English • What course are you taking this semester? • I'm a student • I graduated last year • I'm in graduate school now • I like to study • Where's the administration building? • You've got to go to the library and do some research • I got an "A" on my paper • I studied all night • Where's my pocket calculator? • I loaned out my typewriter • My roommate can't sleep while I'm typing • I have a question • Did you ask him? • The teacher asked me a lot of questions • No talking during the test • We have a test tomorrow • Close/open your books • Begin/stop writing • I lost my pencil • Your writing is terrible • Please don't erase the board • Did you pass or fail? • Any questions? • You haven't turned in your paper to me yet • She and I discussed it • Let's take a break • When you've been absent, you must bring an excuse • Additional vocabulary words

10. FOOD AND DRINK   **191**

Have you eaten? • I haven't eaten yet • He eats too much • Are you hungry? • Let's go to a restaurant • What are you going to order? • Do you want a cocktail? • Do you want red or white wine? • I'll have a scotch and water • I want a tall Coke/Pepsi • Do you want a soft drink? • They have a lot of different beers • He never drinks whiskey • I like sandwiches and hamburgers • Where's the waiter/waitress? • The service is lousy • I've been waiting 20 minutes • I want a large/medium/small milk • I'll have iced/hot tea • I'll have coffee after I eat • Do you want milk/cream and sugar? • I take it black, please • Sugar only/both, please • The meat is too rare • The vegetables are overdone • The food is delicious • Additional vocabulary words

11. CLOTHING   **215**

I have to go shopping • What are you wearing tonight? • The dress is an odd color • Do you have any dirty clothes? • I need to do some laundry • Is there a laundromat nearby? • He always dresses nicely • The shirt and tie don't match • Blue agrees with you • My trousers are torn • Can you sew on a button for me? • I can't tie a bow tie • Most women wear slacks nowadays • Shirt and shoes are required • I wear shorts every day in the summer • I need to wash out my shirt • Your socks don't match • Who took my hat? • I can't fasten my belt • When I took my coat to the cleaners, it shrunk

12. SPORTS AND RECREATION   **226**

Do you like to play baseball? • I run every day • I enjoy going to the mountains to fish • Can you ski? • I went camping last summer • I can roller-skate, but I've never tried ice-skating • We went canoeing every day • He has a sailboat • She's an expert surfer • I don't like to swim in the ocean • Many people hunt in the fall • He's crazy about betting on the horses • She loves to ride horses • He hopes to compete in the Olympics • I hate calisthenics • What do you do in your spare time? • Do you like to dance? • Do you want to learn to dance? • Let's stop and rest now • I go bowling every week • Additional vocabulary words

13. TRAVEL 239

Someday I'm going to Africa • Have you ever been to Japan? • I'm flying to New York tonight • Are your bags packed? • I'll take you to the airport • Which airline are you taking? • What time does the plane take off? • Do you have your ticket? • May I see your ticket, please? • The airport is closed due to fog • The flight has been delayed an hour • The flight has been canceled • I have to change planes in Chicago • There's a two-hour layover • The seats are not reserved • The plane is ready for boarding now • Have you checked your luggage? • Please fasten your seat belt • Would you like a magazine or newspaper? • We will land in ten minutes • Is somebody meeting you? • I enjoy riding a train • What time does the bus arrive? • What time does the train leave? • Have you bought your ticket? • I'm going to the hotel to take a bath • How long are you staying? • The elevator is stuck • Do you have a car? • Can you drive? • I don't have a license • Do you know how to use a manual shift? • It's illegal to park here overnight • Slow down and make a right turn • Make a left turn and stop • Would you call me a cab, please? • Come and visit me sometime • Additional vocabulary words

14. ANIMALS, COLORS 267

15. CIVICS 274

I'm a Democrat/Republican/Independent • I voted, did you? • Who's the new president? • Who won the election? • The legislature/congress is responsible for passing laws • She is a congresswoman • He is a senator/judge/lawyer • We must pay taxes to support the government • Our country is large • I had to pay a parking fine • Which city is the capitol? • If you break the law, you might go to jail • If you disobey the law, you will be punished • You must obey the law • The police arrested him for speeding • She plans to sue them • They are on strike against the company • Last year the students protested • I was on the picket line all morning • I move we pass it • I second the motion • Did you receive a notification to appear in court? Do you belong to the P.T.A.? • He's on Social Security • She gets Supplementary Salary Income • If you go to court, you should have a good lawyer

16. RELIGION 290

Are you a Christian? • Judaism is an old religion • Are you a Roman Catholic or a Protestant? • He's an atheist • Have you been baptized? • I go to church every Sunday • Jewish people go to temple on the Sabbath • Which church do you belong to? • He used to be a preacher • She's a missionary • Do you want me to interpret the sermon? • Additional vocabulary words

17. NUMBERS, TIME, DATES, AND MONEY 302

Do you have a TTY? • What's your number? • My phone number is _____ • It is 4:45 • It is 6:15 • It is ten till nine • He is 87 years old • I was born in 1911 • My birthday is April 3, 1948 • I'll see you next Monday • I visited my aunt two months ago • I bought a new house two years ago • I graduate in two years • I pay every three months • He goes to the movies every Tuesday • I see her every Saturday • The fourth of July is a holiday • Have a nice Thanksgiving • Merry Christmas • Happy Hanukkah • Happy New Year • Happy birthday • How much does the book cost? • Have you a nickel/dime/quarter? • Can you change a five? • How much did you pay? • It is under/over five dollars • I paid less than you • I have no money • I'm broke • How much does it cost to get in? • How much does he owe? • Additional vocabulary words

APPENDIX: THE MANUAL ALPHABET 336
DICTIONARY/INDEX 342

Preface to the Revised Edition

Since the publication of the first edition of this book, new techniques for teaching American Sign Language (ASL) have been developed, and more information about the grammar of ASL has been discovered. This second edition incorporates some of this information. Also, I felt that some of my explanations of the grammar of ASL needed amplification, so I have added new material and revised some of the old.

Knowing how difficult it is to learn signs from drawings, I decided to make videotapes that illustrate all of the sentences and signs. These are available from Sign Media, Inc., 4020 Blackburn Lane, Burtonsville, MD 20866; phone: (301) 421-0268, fax: (301) 421-0270. If your budget will not permit the purchase of the tapes, you might ask your local library to purchase them, thus making them available to everyone in your community. I hope the study of ASL will bring you the pleasure and satisfaction it has brought to thousands of others.

—Lou Fant
January 1994

1

How to Use This Book

American Sign Language, commonly abbreviated to ASL and occasionally known as Ameslan, is the sign language most deaf people use when they are communicating among themselves. It has its own grammatical structure, which differs from English grammar. You must approach ASL in the same manner you would approach any foreign language—do not expect ASL to be like English or to conform to rules of English grammar.* Do not ask why ASL, or any language, has a certain structure; ask only how it works. It does no good at all to ask Spanish-speaking people, for example, why they put adjectives after nouns; they just do, and you must accept that. Some of the constructions in ASL may seem odd to you at first because they depart radically from the way we say things in English, but after a while they will seem as natural as English.

It is a common misconception that ASL is merely the finger-spelling of English words. Fingerspelling—using the manual al-

---

*For a more detailed discussion of the grammatical structure of ASL, see Chapter 2, "A Guide to American Sign Language."

phabet to spell out entire words letter by letter—is occasionally incorporated into ASL, but the vocabulary of ASL consists of signs. (See the Appendix for a complete treatment of this manual alphabet.)

The format of this book is not that of a traditional foreign language textbook. There are no formal grammatical exercises or drills, and there are no vocabulary lists to memorize. Rather, this book is a guide to conversation with deaf people. It contains phrases, expressions, sentences, and questions that come up in casual, everyday conversations. These phrases enable you to begin talking with deaf people without first having to master the grammar of the language.

Chapter 2, "A Guide to American Sign Language," covers the major components of ASL grammar. Not a complete grammar of ASL, the guide is intended to help you better understand the structure of the sentences in this book. It is not necessary, however, to understand the grammatical structure before you begin signing those sentences. You may skip over the chapter on grammar and go directly to the sentences and begin signing. As you become more proficient in ASL, you will want to create your own sentences, and then you will need to study the ASL guide. At this stage, the Dictionary/Index will also be helpful to you in locating the signs you want to use in your own expressions.

Chapters 3 through 17 cover the basic topics that occur in the ordinary course of our lives. (The chapter on health also includes some expressions that are needed in emergency situations.) These 15 chapters are self-contained and do not need to be employed in any particular order. You may begin wherever you like, choosing whichever subject you wish, and be able to proceed without having read the previous chapters. If you are seeking quick access to the rudiments of language for your first conversations with a deaf person, though, the chapters entitled "Everyday Expressions," "Signing and Deafness," and "Getting Acquainted" might be the best ones to begin with.

This book can be used not only as an instant reference manual but also as a study guide should you wish to become fluent in ASL. If you do wish to assimilate the phrases, the most efficient way to use this book is to study one chapter thoroughly, practicing the sentences until you can do them without looking at the pictures. The next step is to use them immediately in conversation. This will help fix them in your memory. To become fluent in ASL, it is important to study and converse in a regular, consistent manner. Do not be afraid of making mistakes, for everyone errs while learning a new language. Deaf people do not expect perfection and usually will cheerfully help you correct your errors.

SIGN LABELS

To enable us to talk about the signs of ASL each sign has been given a name, or label. We use English words for these labels. In this book the labels appear beneath the picture of the sign. People often confuse the meaning of a sign with its label, but a sign may have several meanings and the label is only one of its meanings. English labels for signs merely provide us with a convenient way of designating which sign we want to talk about or which sign to use.

Let's look at an example. The word *run* has numerous meanings in English. Some of them are:

He *runs* fast.
My nose *runs*.
There's a *run* on the stock market
She's *running* for office.
He scored a *run*.
You stocking has a *run* in it.

Figure 1. RUN

The sign labeled RUN (Figure 1) could be used only in the first example above, for that is the only meaning of that sign. Each of the other examples requires a different sign.

A sign label does not tell you how a sign may be used to express meanings quite different from the label. Take for example the sign FINISH (Figures 2, 3).

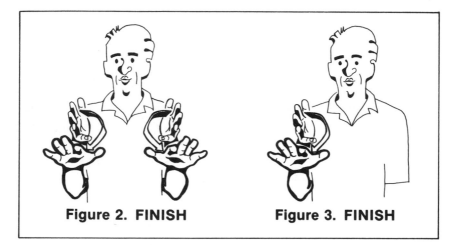

Figure 2. FINISH   Figure 3. FINISH

The sign phrase EAT FINISH may mean: (1) ate, eaten; (2) already eat, already eaten; (3) did eat; or (4) done eating (Figures 4, 5).

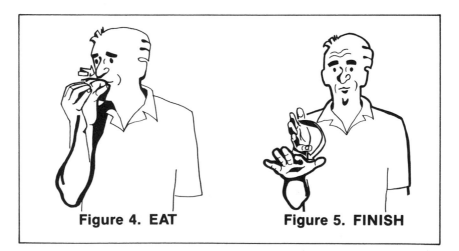

Figure 4. EAT   Figure 5. FINISH

In this signed sentence, WORK FINISH GO TO HOME (Figures 6–9), the FINISH sign indicates that when one act is over, another follows. This sentence would translate as "After work I am going home," "After work I went home," or "When work is done, I am going home."

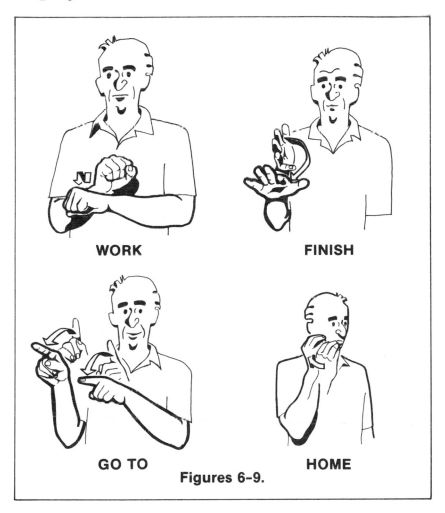

WORK   **FINISH**

GO TO   **HOME**

Figures 6–9.

One form of the FINISH sign by itself can mean "That's enough!," "Stop it!," or "I/She/He did already!" (Figure 10).

The FINISH sign offers an excellent example of the danger of confusing a sign label with the meaning of the sign. Obviously this sign means much more than merely "finish."

Figure 10. FINISH!

When using the Dictionary/Index at the back of this book to find a sign you want to use, be sure you look for the sign that matches the meaning of the word you have in mind. Do not look just for the English word itself. For example, if you want the sign for "run" in the sense that someone is running for office, you will have to think of "competing," "contesting," or "racing" in order to locate the correct sign (COMPETE, Figure 11).

Figure 11. COMPETE

READING THE DRAWINGS

The pictures are to be read from left to right when they are read as a sentence. However, an individual sign may sometimes require more than one picture to illustrate it, and will sometimes be read from right to left. Five types of aids are provided to help you know which way to read a drawing, and thus form the sign correctly.

The Five Aids for Reading the Drawings

The first aid is the use of both *bold* (dark-lined) and *light-lined* drawings. The bold-lined drawings show the final position of the sign. The light-lined drawings show the first and, if necessary, additional positions of the sign. In the sign labeled DELICIOUS (Figure 12), for example, the light-lined drawing shows the middle finger touching the lips. The bold-lined drawing shows the hand turned outward. These are the first and final positions, respectively. Always remember that the bold-lined drawing shows the final position of the sign.

Figure 12. DELICIOUS   **Figure 13. DAY**

The second aid is the use of several kinds of *arrows*, which show exactly how the hands move in forming a sign. The sign DAY (Figure 13), for example, is formed by moving the arm from the first position (light-lined) to the final position (bold-lined), following the movement indicated by the arrow.

Repetitive movement is shown by the use of a bent arrow, as in the signs HAPPY (Figure 14) and FOOTBALL (Figure 15). This means you do the same movement twice.

Figure 14. HAPPY   **Figure 15. FOOTBALL**

Swerving movement is shown by a twisted arrow, as in the sign labeled NEVER (Figure 16).

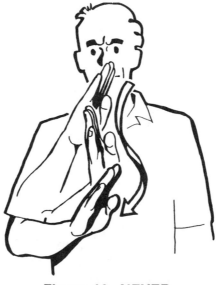

Figure 16. NEVER

Circular movement is shown by a circular arrow, as in the signs COFFEE (Figure 17) and GOING (Figure 18).

Figure 17. COFFEE   **Figure 18. GOING**

The arrows in the sign CAR (Figure 19) show the hands repeating a movement, but in opposite directions. The sign looks as if you were steering a car.

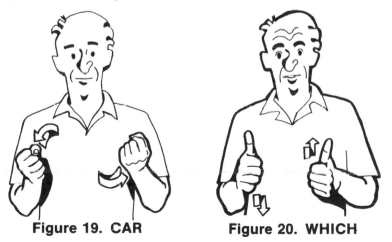

Figure 19. CAR   **Figure 20. WHICH**

In the sign WHICH (Figure 20), the arrows indicate that the hands move alternately. As the left hand goes up, the right hand goes down. Then both hands reverse their directions (left: down; right: up), then they reverse again going in their original directions.

The same thing applies to the sign CONTROL (Figure 21) as does to the WHICH sign, but *numbers*, the third aid, have been added to help you see more clearly where the hands begin and end. When both hands are in their number one positions, the right hand is farther out from the chest than the left. The arrows show that the right hand moves backward, and the left hand moves forward, reversing their positions. The arrows then show that the hands reverse positions again as the hands move to the third position. (Note that both the first and third positions are shown in bold-lines since that is the final, as well as the beginning, position. This will occur only rarely, but if in doubt, look at the numbers. The sign looks as if you are guiding a horse with the reins.

Figure 21. CONTROL

The arrows together with the numbers in Figure 22 (HAMBURGER) show a reversal of position here. In the first position the right hand is on top, and in the second position it is on bottom.

Figure 22. HAMBURGER

A *broken arrow*, the fourth aid, is shown in Figure 23 (TREES) along with the circular arrows that show how the hand moves from first to final position. The broken arrow means that there may be two or three repetitions of the sign. The sign is repeated (third and fourth positions) only once in the drawing.

Figure 23. TREES

The *squiggles* in Figure 24 (WAIT) are the fifth aid, and they tell you to wriggle the fingers. In the sign for "13" (Figure 25), they tell you to wriggle the index and second finger together, but not the rest of the hand.

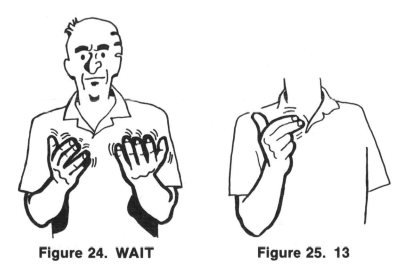

Figure 24. WAIT   **Figure 25. 13**

The Angle of the Pictures

In most of the drawings the signer is shown facing directly front, but many signs can best be learned by seeing the sign from an angle slightly off center; thus, the signer is sometimes shown facing slightly to his right or to his left. The WANT sign (Figure 26), for instance, would be difficult to read if it were shown

Figure 26. WANT

straight on, so the signer is shown facing slightly to his right to give you a clearer view of the sign. When you make the sign, however, do not turn to your right, but make it straight toward the person to whom you are signing. In a few of the drawings, such as those for LESSON (Figures 27 and 28), the signer is shown from a rear view, as well as from the front, to help you to see the sign more clearly.

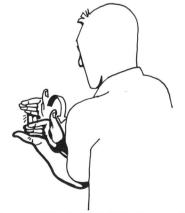

Figure 27. LESSON   **Figure 28. LESSON (rear view)**

Labeling of the Drawings

When more than one drawing is required to illustrate how a single sign is made, each sign label is followed by a number. For example, the illustration of the sign AWFUL requires two steps, and these are labeled "AWFUL (1)," and "AWFUL (2):"

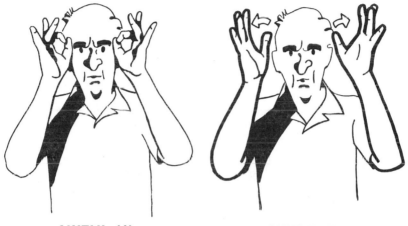

AWFUL (1)   **AWFUL (2)**

When a single concept can be signed in more than one way, several possible signs are shown, and their labels are followed by a letter. For example, the three separate ways to sign BAPTIZE are labeled "BAPTIZE (A)," "BAPTIZE (B)," and "BAPTIZE (C):"

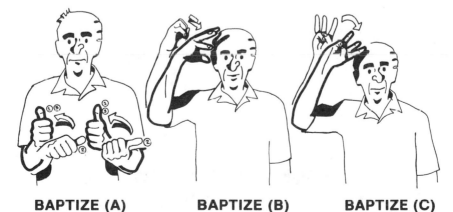

BAPTIZE (A)   **BAPTIZE (B)**   **BAPTIZE (C)**

Sometimes, an entire phrase or sentence can be said in more than one way. In these cases, each sentence, along with its component signs, is shown and indicated with a letter. For example, the sentence "Why didn't you eat last night?" can be signed as "PAST NIGHT YOU EAT NOT WHY" or as "PAST NIGHT WHY YOU EAT NOT:"

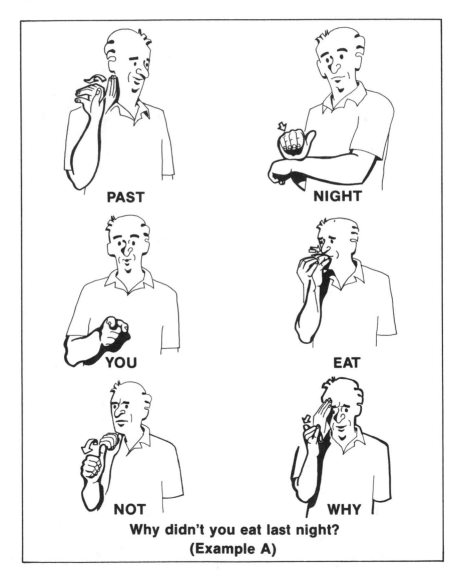

PAST　　**NIGHT**

YOU　　**EAT**

NOT　　**WHY**

Why didn't you eat last night?
(Example A)

PAST

NIGHT

WHY

YOU

EAT

NOT

Why didn't you eat last night?
(Example B)

FACIAL EXPRESSIONS

We have given our cartoon character various facial expressions to emphasize the importance of facial expressions in ASL. The expressions are by no means the same all the time. The same sign will require different expressions at different times, depending upon the feeling you wish to convey.

SOME DOS AND DON'TS

Try to avoid any bright light shining directly into the face of the person watching you. Bright lights are to deaf people what noise is to hearing people.

To get a deaf person's attention, gently touch the person on the shoulder. If the person is too far away to touch, wave your arm. Deaf people also get each others' attention by stamping their feet on a wooden floor or by turning a light switch off and on, but it is not recommended that hearing people do this. The manner in which these are done carry subtle meanings that are learned only with years of experience. If you stamped too hard or flashed the light too vigorously, for example, it might mean an emergency situation exists, which, if there really were no emergency, could lead to feelings of consternation.

Make sure you do not stand or sit in the middle of someone else's conversation. This often happens in a crowded room or when two deaf people are seated far apart from each other.

Avoid such nervous behavior as drumming your fingers on a table or tapping your shoe on the floor. If you do such things, the deaf person will constantly turn to look at you to see what you want. Deaf people are extra-sensitive to vibrations, so avoid making unnecessary ones.

2

A Guide to American Sign Language

In the United States there are several sign systems that should not be confused with American Sign Language (ASL). These systems are ways of putting the English language into a manual-visual form; thus, they are called systems of Manually Coded English (MCEs). They are designed primarily for the purpose of teaching English to deaf children. An MCE uses the same signs that are used in ASL plus many new signs that have been created to serve special functions that do not exist in ASL. In an MCE the signs are arranged in accordance with the rules of English grammar. ASL, on the other hand, is not a way of coding English, but rather a language in and of itself. It differs from English in many respects. This book is concerned solely with ASL.

LIGHT, SIGHT, AND SPACE

Most languages are based entirely on sounds, and herein lies the unique difference between spoken language and ASL. Instead of sound waves in the form of spoken words, ASL uses light waves in the form of signs. ASL is a visual-spatial language. One *sees* ASL, and hearing plays absolutely no part in it. Because of this, ASL consists not only of signs made with the hands but also of facial expressions, head movements, body movements, and an efficient use of the space around the signer. (In ASL the person "speaking" is the *signer*, and the person "listening" is the *watcher*, *observer*, or *reader*.) ASL is not mime, although mime sometimes is incorporated into the language.

The Sight Line

We begin the study of ASL with an understanding of how space is used. Imagine a line extending from the center of the signer's chest, straight out, parallel to the floor. This imaginary line is called the *sight line*. The sight line divides all space into the right or left side.

The Sight Line

Whenever the signer turns the body, the sight line moves with it.

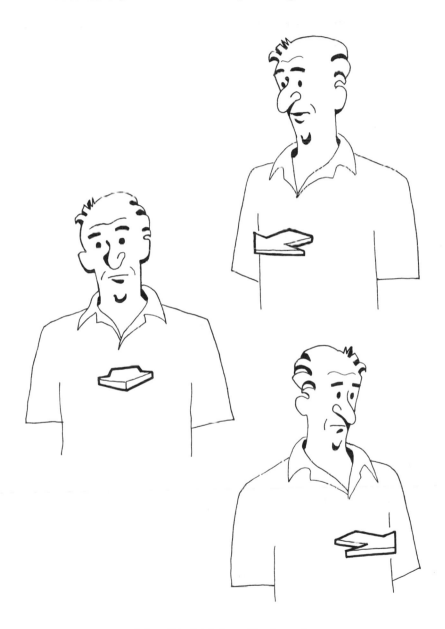

The Sight Line (3 views)

One of the most frequently used signs is a simple point with the index finger. When the signer points parallel to the sight line toward the watcher, it means "you." When the signer points to his or her own chest, it means "I" or "me." When the signer points to the right or the left of the sight line it means "he," "she," or "it."

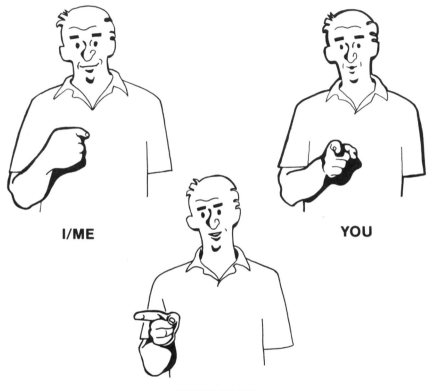

I/ME   **YOU**

HE/SHE/IT

Placement of Signs

People, places, objects, and events may be established or placed to the right and left of the sight line. Once this is done, the signer merely points to that space when reference to it is made. For example, as on page 21, suppose the signer tells the watcher, "I saw your father yesterday. He was driving a new car." The signer makes the sign for "see" toward the right.* This movement tells the

---

*Or toward the left, if the signer is left-handed.

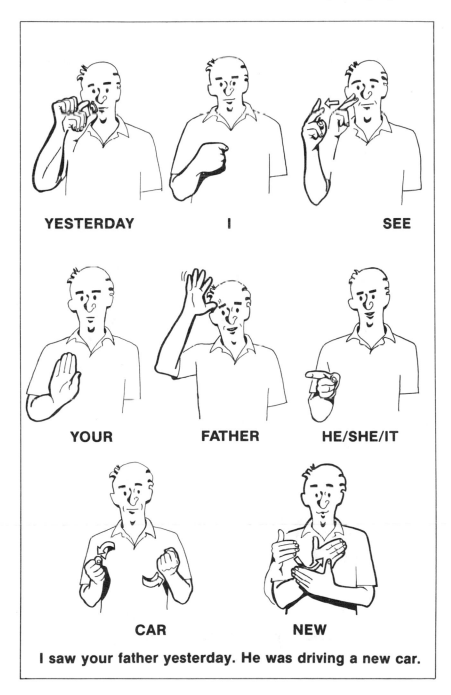

YESTERDAY   I   SEE

YOUR   FATHER   HE/SHE/IT

CAR   NEW

I saw your father yesterday. He was driving a new car.

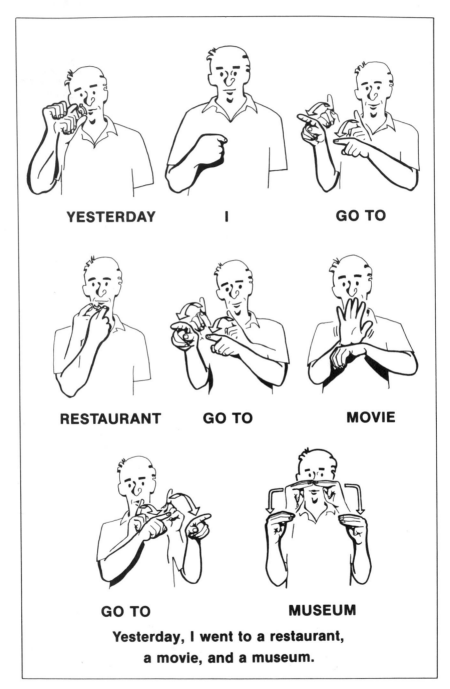

YESTERDAY   I   GO TO

RESTAURANT   GO TO   MOVIE

GO TO   MUSEUM

**Yesterday, I went to a restaurant,
a movie, and a museum.**

watcher that the signer is about to say something about someone. Then the signer signs "father," and that tells the watcher who the someone is. The watcher also now knows that "father" occupies that space to the right of the sight line because the SEE sign moved toward that space. The signer may now point right, and it means "he," and it will continue to mean "he" (father) until the signer places someone or something else in that space.

Placement of more than one person, place, or object in the same space at the same time may not be done, but placement in other spaces at the same time may be done. For example, as on page 22, the signer may say, "Yesterday I went to a restaurant, a movie, and a museum." The three places are set up in three different spaces. Notice that the restaurant is nearer the signer, and the movie is farther out. Both may be to the right of the sight line, but they occupy slightly different spaces.

Avoid placing persons on the sight line itself. This space, with some exceptions, is reserved for the watcher. Any signs that move on or along the sight line have to do with the watcher, and no one else may occupy this area. An exception to this rule is illustrated by the following example:

BOOK   **HAVE**   **HE/SHE/IT**   **LIKE**
I have a book. It is interesting.

The signer first establishes the book, then points to it. When placing things on the sight line that have no reference to the watcher, place them near the signer and be sure to point to that space.

FACIAL EXPRESSIONS

In a spoken language, the rise and fall of the voice adds meaning to the words spoken. The various ways one can say "I love you" illustrate the importance of vocal inflection. The characteristic rising of the voice toward the end of a question is another example. In ASL, the face has these duties and supplies additional subtleties and nuances of meaning. Signs have meanings in and of themselves, just as words do, but these meanings are altered, shaped, enriched, and amplified by facial expressions. A face that is devoid of expression is to a deaf person the equivalent of a monotone speaker—boring and difficult to follow.

Facial expressions in ASL are especially important when asking questions. In general, when one asks a wh- sign question (who, what, why, where, when, which, and how) the eyebrows usually go downward.

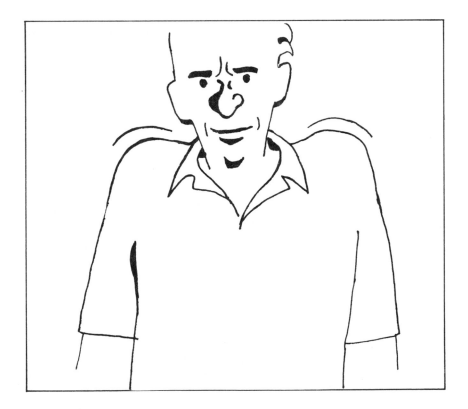

All other questions usually cause the eyebrows to move upward.

These are not rigid rules, and you may sometimes see something different, but these rules do generally apply. That the eyebrows will move up or down, however, is a certainty when asking questions.

The signer must learn to be expressive with the eyes and mouth as well as with the eyebrows. The eyes will open wide or squint to narrow slits; the mouth will open and close; the lips will purse and stretch; the cheeks will puff out; and even the tongue will sometimes protrude.

BODY LANGUAGE

Body language is an essential element of ASL. Information is communicated not only by the face but also by the head, shoulders, torso, legs, and feet. The head may tilt forward, back, or to the side, especially when questions are asked.

For additional practice in facial expressions, body language, and the use of the hands to express ideas and convey information, I suggest the book and videotapes produced by Gilbert Eastman entitled *From Mime to Sign.* These may be purchased from the Gallaudet University Bookstore, 800 Florida Avenue NE, Washington, DC, 20002-3625; phone: (202) 651-5380.

The shoulders may shrug; the body may bend forward and back-ward and twist.

The incorporation of the whole body into the expression of sign language is absolutely required for clear, understandable communication. It is possible, of course, to overdo the matter, but it is better to err on the side of doing too much than too little. Deaf people are often described as animated, alive, vibrant, etc. This is due to their mastery of body language. For successful communication, you must do likewise.

PAST, PRESENT, FUTURE

One of the most difficult tasks in learning a new language is conjugating verbs in their various tenses. The struggle with regular and irregular verbs tries the student's patience to the utmost. It is, therefore, a pleasure to inform you that such is not the case with ASL. Learning to place actions in the past or future is comparatively simple.

No tenses are incorporated in the signs themselves. Tense is conveyed by using signs that tell when an action takes place, and these particular signs are called *time indicators*. In English, for example, one may say, "I saw you." In ASL, the sign SEE is always made the same way whether it means "see," "sees," "seeing," "saw," or "seen":

SEE

In order to sign the equivalent of "I saw you," it is necessary to use a time indicator. One may use signs that will place the event in a specific time, such as "yesterday," "last night," or "this morning."

YESTERDAY   **I**   **SEE**

Yesterday, I saw.

PAST   **NIGHT**   **I**   **SEE**

Last night, I saw.

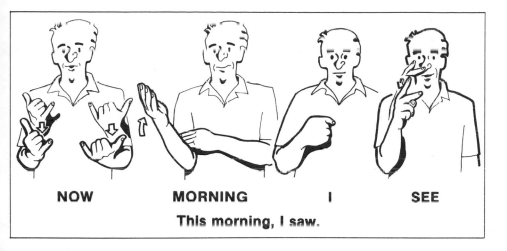

NOW   MORNING   I   SEE

This morning, I saw.

One may also use the FINISH sign to indicate no specific time, simply the past:

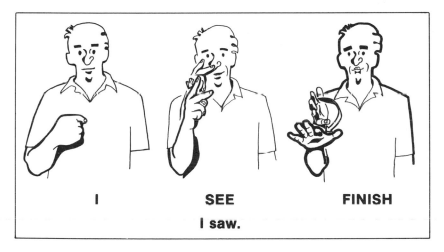

I   SEE   FINISH

I saw.

The PAST sign may be used instead of the FINISH sign, which conveys slightly more information.

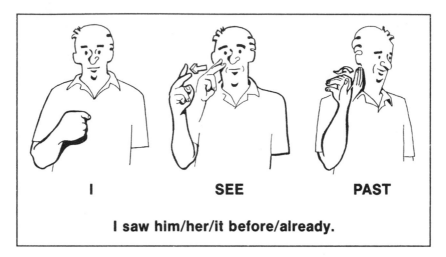

| I | SEE | PAST |

I saw him/her/it before/already.

The use of a time indicator also applies to the future tense.

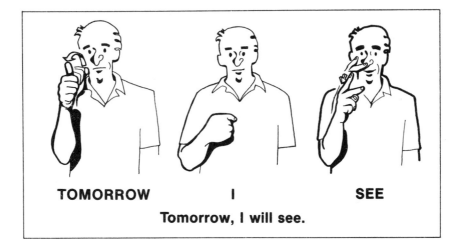

| TOMORROW | I | SEE |

Tomorrow, I will see.

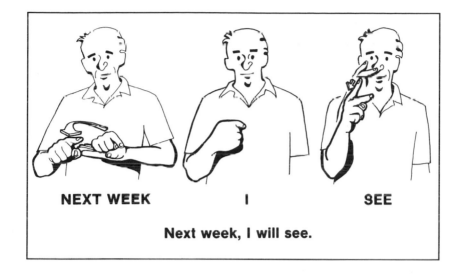

NEXT WEEK   **I**   **SEE**

Next week, I will see.

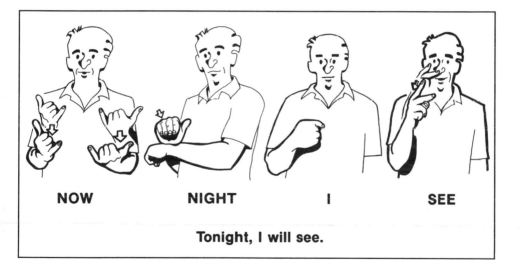

NOW   **NIGHT**   **I**   **SEE**

Tonight, I will see.

The previous phrases illustrate placing the event in a specific future time. For a nonspecific future time, use the WILL sign.

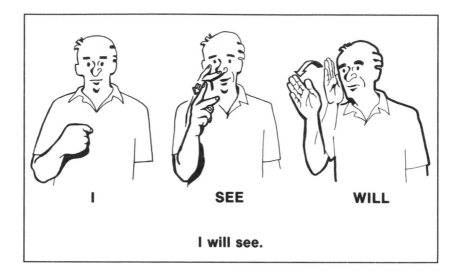

I   SEE   WILL

I will see.

Notice that nonspecific time indicators such as FINISH and WILL usually follow the verb; however, they may come before the verb as well. Specific time indicators, on the other hand, always come at the beginning of a statement.

Context is used a great deal in ASL when establishing or determining tense. For instance, the signer may tell the watcher about an incident that occurred some time in the past or that will occur in the future. The signer will first establish the time of the incident by using a time indicator sign; then the signer will never repeat the time indicator sign or use any additional ones. The watcher knows that all the events described by the signer occur in the time frame established at the beginning of the statement by the time indicator sign used.

VERB DIRECTIONALITY

Verbs in ASL fall into three categories: non-directional verbs, one-directional verbs, and multi-directional verbs. Movement in verb signs may express who is performing an action (the subject) and to whom the action is directed (the direct object). This quality of movement is called verb directionality.

The non-directional verbs do not express either subject or direct object; therefore, these two things (subject and direct object nouns and pronouns) must be supplied.

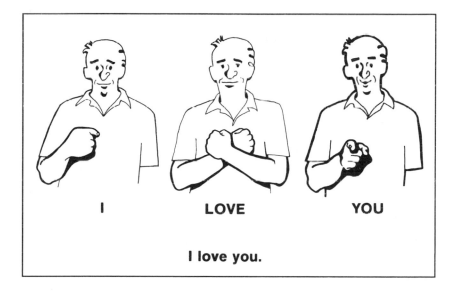

I   LOVE   YOU

I love you.

The verbs LOVE, UNDERSTAND, and WANT in the sentences here and on the next page do obviously have movement in them, but that movement does not express either subject or direct object;

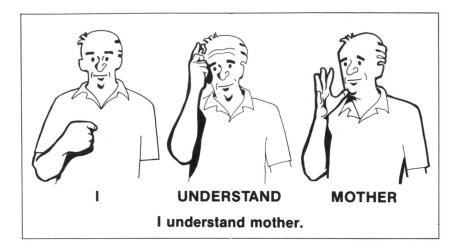

I   UNDERSTAND   MOTHER

I understand mother.

HE/SHE/IT   WANT   CAR

She wants a car.

that is, the movement has no directionality. Subject and direct object signs must be supplied.

One-directional verb signs express direct object but not subject, as in these sentences.

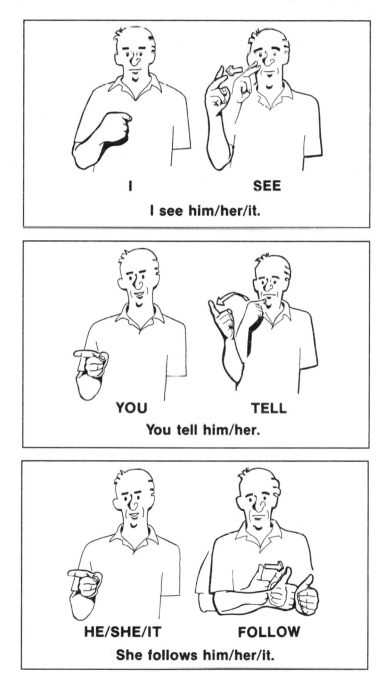

I   **SEE**

I see him/her/it.

YOU   **TELL**

You tell him/her.

HE/SHE/IT   **FOLLOW**

She follows him/her/it.

One-directional verbs move toward the direct object; thus, a noun or pronoun is not required. The exception to this rule occurs when the signer is the direct object. For example, "You see me" must be signed:

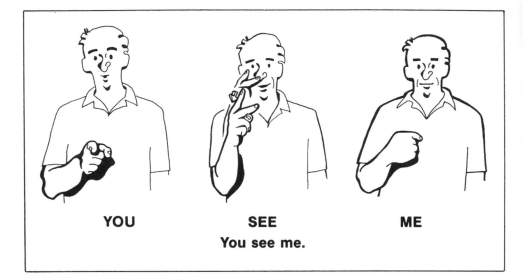

YOU   **SEE**   **ME**

You see me.

The direct object here is the signer ("me"), and since the movement of the SEE sign does not move toward the direct object, then the direct object must be signed. Notice also that the SEE sign does indeed move slightly to the right of the sight line, not directly toward the watcher.

The movement of multi-directional signs expresses both subject and direct object. The sign moves from the subject toward the direct object; thus, neither the subject nor direct object is signed. Examples:

HELP
I help you.*

HELP
He helps me.

HELP
He helps her.

---

*In this illustration, the body is faced to your left to give you a better view of how the sign is made, but the sign itself goes along the sight line from the signer to the watcher.

The movement from a space normally implies that whoever occupies that space is the subject. The movement toward a space normally implies that whoever occupies that space is the direct object.

TO BE OR NOT TO BE

Many sentences in English require some form of the "to be" verb. Examples of such sentences include "I am fine," "You are tired," "Where is Joe?," and "They were not here." There is no "to be" verb in ASL. The above examples are signed, "I FINE," "YOU TIRED," "WHERE JOE?," and "THEY NOT HERE." Statements such as "It is raining," "The flower is growing," and "The train is late" are signed:

RAIN

It is raining.

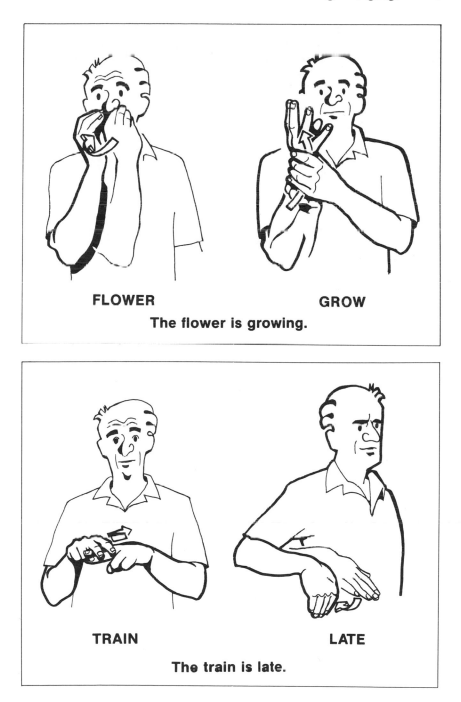

FLOWER   **GROW**

The flower is growing.

TRAIN   **LATE**

The train is late.

When the signer wishes to stress or emphasize statements, then the TRUE sign is used. The following statement means simply that I am sick:

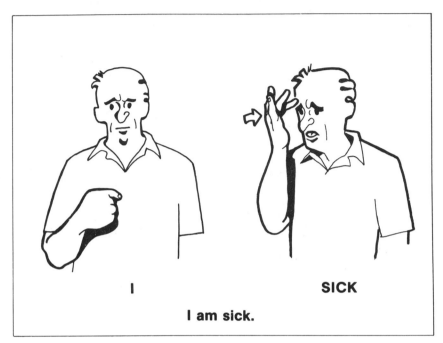

I

SICK

I am sick.

The following statement means that I am really sick, or I am very sick:

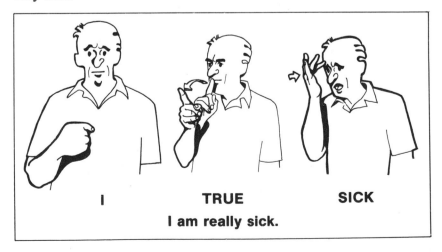

I   **TRUE**   **SICK**

I am really sick.

Do not confuse the use of the TRUE sign as a sign of stress and emphasis with a form of the "to be" verb in English.

The TRUE sign also means true, truly, real, really, sure, surely, certainly, indeed, and actually. When used alone with a questioning expression, the TRUE sign means "Is that so?" or "Are you sure?"

WORDS VERSUS SIGNS

A word stands for a concept or an idea. If someone says "tree," you understand immediately because you have in your mind the concept of tree. The same applies to signs. If the signer signs TREE, the watcher understands it immediately without having to think the word "tree." In other words, a sign stands for an idea or concept; it does not stand for a word.

When you form statements in ASL, do not try to find a sign for every word in the English statement. Languages do not work that way. (For example, in English one says, "I am hungry," but in Spanish and French one says, "I have hunger." In ASL one says, "I hunger.") First get clearly in mind the ideas you want to communicate, forget the words, and then find the appropriate signs to express the ideas.

MAKING STATEMENTS

Language is made up of utterances or statements. In spoken languages the statements consist of words, but in ASL the statements consist of signs and fingerspelling. There are two kinds of statements, those that ask questions and those that do not ask questions. Let's look at how these statements are formed in ASL.

STATEMENTS THAT ASK QUESTIONS

1. Yes/No Questions: These are such questions as, "Are you hungry?" and "You want to go to the movies?" This type of question is usually accompanied by the types of head tilts shown on pages 27 and 28 and by raised eyebrows as shown on page 25. The eyebrows are not *always* raised but generally they are.

HUNGER **YOU**

Are you hungry?

MOVIE **GO TO** **WANT**

Do you want to go to the movies?

WH SIGN QUESTIONS

WHO   **WHAT SHRUG**

WHAT   **WHY**

WHERE   **WHEN**

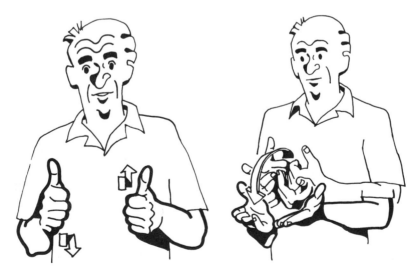

WHICH   **HOW**

2. Wh- Sign Questions: These are the questions that use *who*, *what*, *why*, *where*, *when*, *which*, and *how*, and they require more than a yes/no answer. These questions are also accompanied by one of the head tilts shown on pages 27 and 28 and by lowered eyebrows as shown on page 24. Again, the eyebrows may not always be lowered but generally they are.

The wh- sign may come at the beginning or at the end of a question, or it may appear in both places. If you wish to emphasize a question, place it at the end.

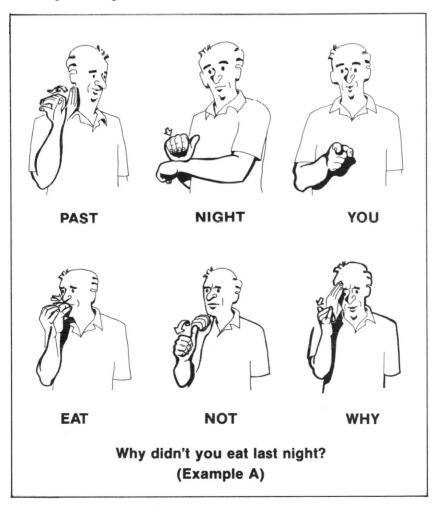

PAST   **NIGHT**   **YOU**

EAT   **NOT**   **WHY**

Why didn't you eat last night?
(Example A)

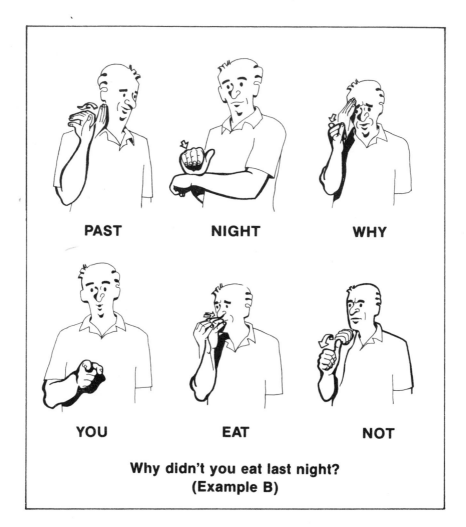

PAST   NIGHT   WHY

YOU   EAT   NOT

Why didn't you eat last night?
(Example B)

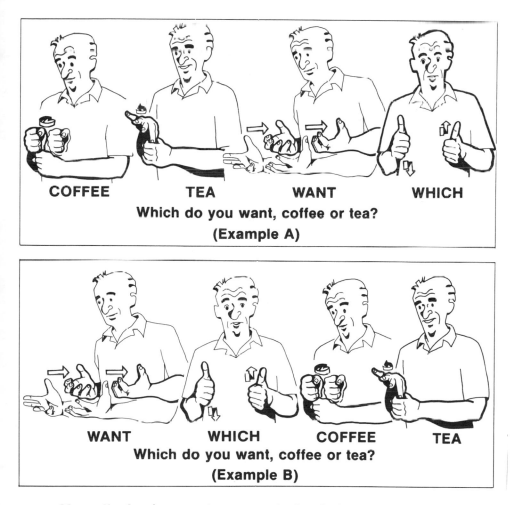

COFFEE TEA WANT WHICH
Which do you want, coffee or tea?
(Example A)

WANT WHICH COFFEE TEA
Which do you want, coffee or tea?
(Example B)

Naturally the signer makes a questioning facial expression when using these wh- sign questions.

Do not use a wh- sign in statements that do not ask questions. In English, for example, we may make such statements as, "When I say 'frog,' jump!" or "Where there is smoke there is fire." In these statements the wh- word does not ask a question; therefore, wh- signs are not used. A different way of making the statement is used.

3. Rhetorical Questions (RHQ): This type of question does not require an answer. For example, "What's in a name?" and "You know why he won't go? I'll tell you why." In English, an RHQ is usually used to set off or emphasize a point, but in ASL it is used much more frequently.

I didn't go because it rained.

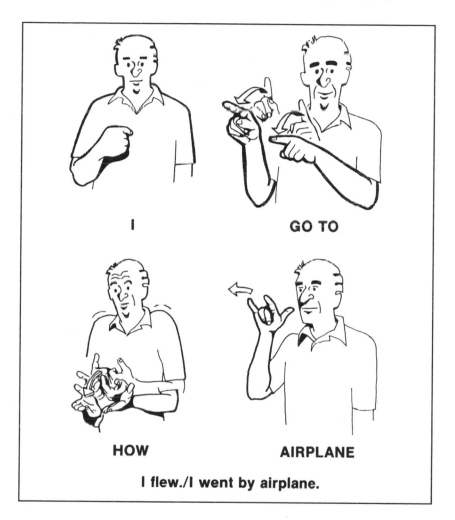

I

GO TO

HOW

AIRPLANE

I flew./I went by airplane.

4. Negative Questions: These are questions such as "Don't you understand?" or "Why didn't you tell me?" Ask them the same way you would a yes/no or a wh- sign question, but put in some form of negation. Usually you just shake your head as you ask the question, but you may add a sign of negation as well.

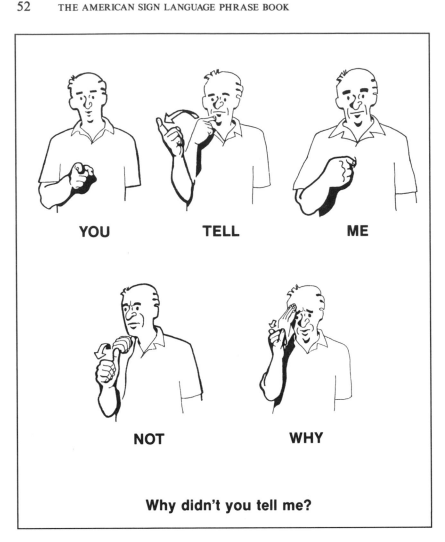

YOU   TELL   ME

NOT   WHY

Why didn't you tell me?

STATEMENTS THAT DO NOT ASK QUESTIONS

1. Simple Statements: These are called "simple" because they are signed exactly the way they are spoken in English. Some examples are "I know you," "You tell me," "He loves you," "She likes movies." They have what is called the subject-verb-object arrangement.

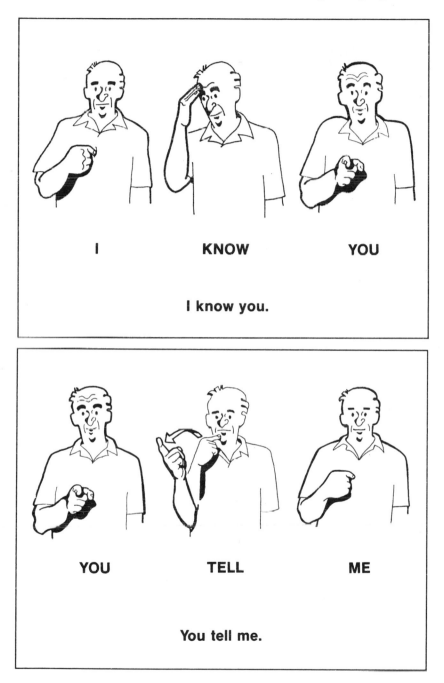

I   KNOW   YOU

I know you.

YOU   TELL   ME

You tell me.

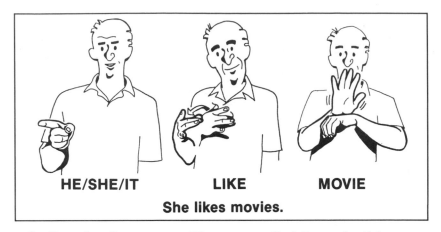

HE/SHE/IT   **LIKE**   **MOVIE**

She likes movies.

2. Complex Statements: These are called "complex" because they involve two objects and are *not* signed exactly the way they are spoken in English. In the statement "You give me the book," the subject is "you," the first object is "me," and the second object is "book."

BOOK   **GIVE ME**

You give me the book.

More explanation about how to make these complex statements is given in the next section, "Stringing the Signs Together."

3. Commands or Requests: The command tells someone to do something. Some examples are "Shut the door!" "Get out of here!" "Keep off the grass!" Generally speaking the signs are made vigorously and are accompanied by a frown (lowered eyebrows).

The request differs from the command only in that it is followed by the sign PLEASE and there is no frown. Some examples are "Bring me a cup of coffee, please," "Turn off the lights, please."

4. Exclamatory Statements: These statements express a strong reaction to something. Some examples are "What!" (surprise), "Ouch!" (pain), "Yahoo!" (elation), "Far out!" (admiration). As in English, these statements usually consist of only one sign in ASL.

STRINGING THE SIGNS TOGETHER

The fascinating part of any language is learning how to put the words together correctly to make a statement. The way words are strung together is the syntax of a language. Except for simple statements, commands, requests, and exclamatory statements, ASL differs considerably from English in syntax.

First, we need to deal with the concept of topicalization, which means that a statement begins with a topic. The topic may be a person, a thing, an action, or an event. In the example used earlier, "I give the book to you," the topic is *the book*. If we topicalize this statement in English, it comes out "The book, I give it to you." Although there is nothing wrong with saying it this way, it sounds awkward to our ears because we are not used to topicalizing in English. The statement "Do you see the woman in the red hat?" if topicalized, comes out "The woman in the red hat, do you see her?" The topic here is *the woman*, a person. "I enjoy going for long walks" comes out "Going for long walks, I enjoy them." Here the topic is *going for long walks*, an activity. "It was a long and difficult test" comes out "The test, it was long and difficult." The topic is *the test*, an event.

The topic of a statement is always followed by the comment. In the above examples, the comments are *I give it to you, in the red hat, I enjoy them*, and *it was long and difficult*.

TOPIC-COMMENT STATEMENTS

To topicalize a statement in ASL, you must first identify the topic and the comment. Because this is something you are not used to doing, it may appear difficult, but with practice it becomes easier. Topic-comment statements fall into one of several categories, which makes them easier to identify. Let's look at these categories.

1. Descriptive Statements: In these statements the topic is described and the description is the comment. An example is "I bought a new, red car." The topic is *car*, the comment is *new, red, I bought*. In ASL, the color of an object usually takes precedence over other qualities, so the comment would be *red, new, I bought*. The signed statement comes out CAR RED NEW BUY ME. (We will talk more later about the pronoun [ME] coming after the verb [BUY].

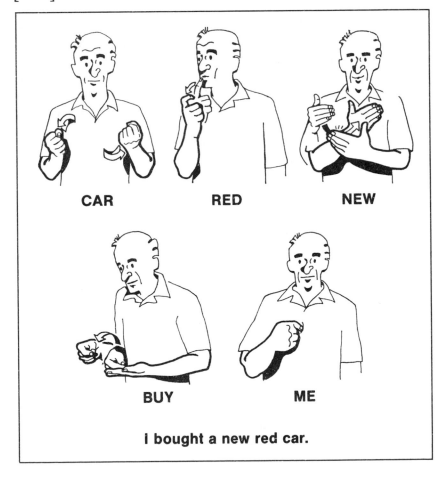

CAR   RED   NEW

BUY   ME

I bought a new red car.

In the statement "I really enjoyed living in that big old house," the topic is *house* and the comment is *big, old, I really enjoyed living there*. In ASL, the size of an object generally comes first, and the emotional reaction comes last (more about this later, too). The statement is signed HOUSE BIG OLD LIVE THERE ENJOY ME TRUE.

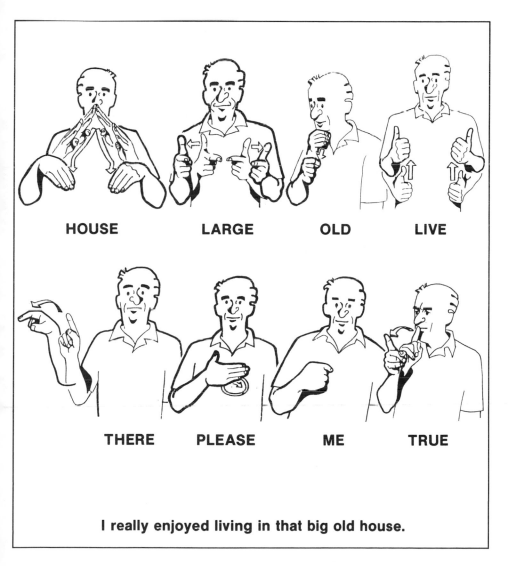

| HOUSE | LARGE | OLD | LIVE |

| THERE | PLEASE | ME | TRUE |

I really enjoyed living in that big old house.

2. Cause and Effect or Stimulus-Reponse Statements: In real life, you cannot have an effect without first having a cause, or a reponse without first having a stimulus. I cannot, for example, scream before a safe falls out of the sky and lands a few feet from me. Neither could I yell "Ouch!" before stubbing my toe on a chair leg. The safe (the cause) must fall first, and the stubbing of my toe (the stimulus) must happen first. The cause/stimulus in these kinds of statements is the topic, the effect/response is the comment.

In the statement "I'm scared of thunder and lightning," the cause/stimulus is *thunder and lightning*, and the effect/response is *scared of.*

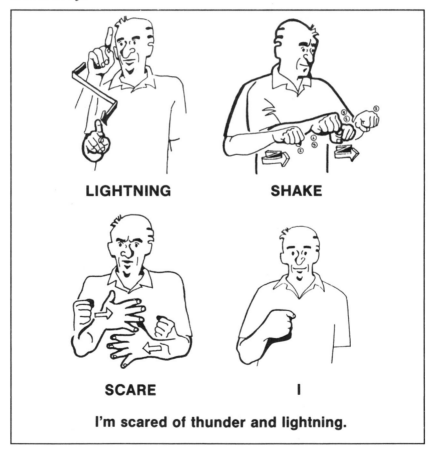

LIGHTNING   **SHAKE**

SCARE   **I**

I'm scared of thunder and lightning.

In the statement "I felt better after I took the medicine," the cause/stimulus is *took the medicine,* and the effect/response is *felt better.*

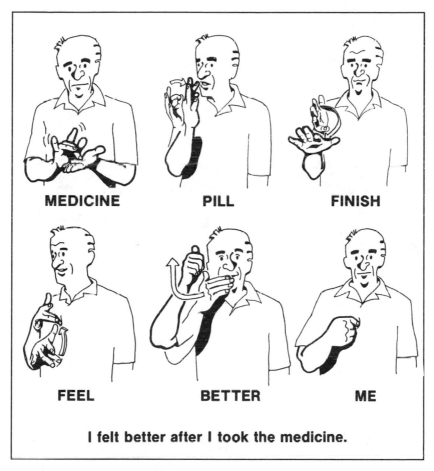

MEDICINE	PILL	FINISH
FEEL	BETTER	ME

I felt better after I took the medicine.

3. Statements That Require Real-Time Sequencing: "Real-time sequencing" means that the events in a statement must be arranged in the chronological order in which they occurred in real life, another way of saying that the cause/stimulus must come before the effect/response.

In the statement "I was happy that no one was hurt when the plane landed safely," the events are not in chronological order.

Rearranged to conform to real-time sequencing, the statement reads, "When the plane landed safely and no one was hurt, I was happy." Picture the scene in your mind as if you were watching it happen. First you see the plane land, then you see everyone get out and that no one is hurt, and then you feel happy.

AIRPLANE LANDING   **SAVE**   **PEOPLE**

PAIN   **NONE**   **HAPPY**   **I**

I was happy that no one was hurt when the plane landed safely.

4. Statements That Move from the General to the Specific: These statements require that you visualize the whole scene, just as you did with the airplane, but this time you move from the large to the small. An example is "There's an old man in the white house on that farm." First see the whole picture of a farm with a white house on it; then move in closer to see an old man in the house.

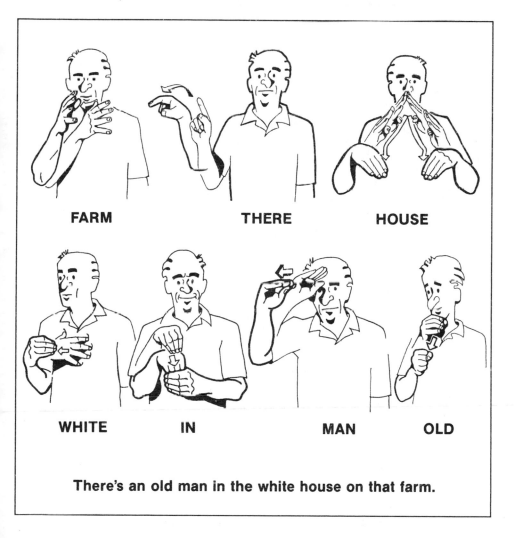

FARM   THERE   HOUSE

WHITE   IN   MAN   OLD

There's an old man in the white house on that farm.

Another example is "I was exhausted by the time I arrived at the hotel in New York." Start with the largest thing, "New York"; then work down to the next largest thing, "hotel." The next largest thing after "hotel" is "you." See yourself arriving at the hotel and then feeling exhausted.

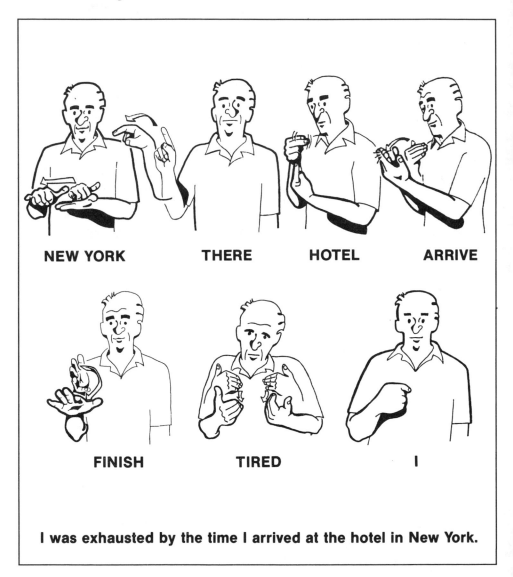

NEW YORK   **THERE**   **HOTEL**   **ARRIVE**

FINISH   **TIRED**   **I**

I was exhausted by the time I arrived at the hotel in New York.

Your success in putting the signs in the correct order, as you probably can tell by now, lies in your ability to imagine, to visualize a scene. ASL is, after all, a visual language, so you must develop this skill.

PRONOUNS

Pronoun signs tend to come before verbs, at the end of statements, and often in both positions. As a rule, they tend to appear at the end of a statement more often than at the beginning, but this rule is honored as much in the breaking as in the keeping of it. As a result, you will not be wrong if you put it in either or both places.

All the pronouns may be expressed by just three hand shapes. The first group is made up of the pointing pronouns. Simply point to get: I, me, you, he, she, him, her, it.

The second group is the posessive pronouns:

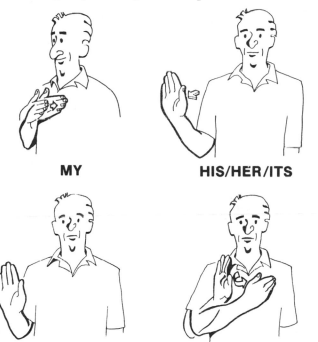

MY   HIS/HER/ITS

YOUR   OUR

The third group is the self pronouns:

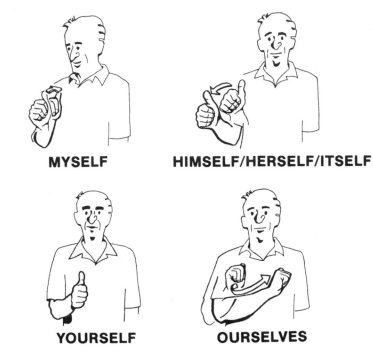

MYSELF　　　　**HIMSELF/HERSELF/ITSELF**

YOURSELF　　　　**OURSELVES**

Third person plural pronouns move in a very small arc:

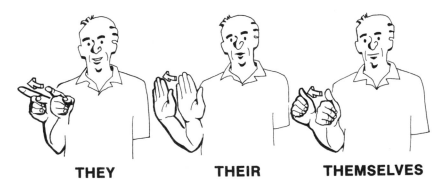

THEY　　　　**THEIR**　　　　**THEMSELVES**

First and second person singular pointing pronouns tend to come at the end of a statement:

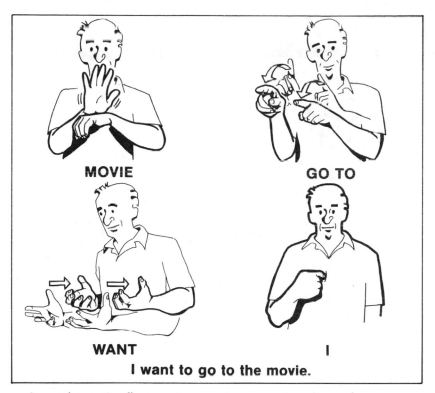

MOVIE

GO TO

WANT

I

I want to go to the movie.

Sometimes the first and second person singular point pronoun is dropped entirely, especially in questions:

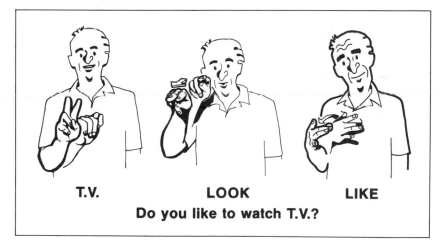

T.V.   **LOOK**   **LIKE**

Do you like to watch T.V.?

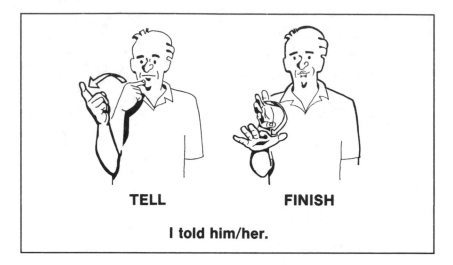

TELL   **FINISH**

I told him/her.

The statement above is a simple declarative statement of fact, so you may assume the subject is "I." If the intent were "You told him," then the sentence would be:

TELL   **FINISH**   **YOU**

You told him/her.

The second person singular pointing pronoun is usually dropped in questions, as on the following page:

TELL   **FINISH**

Did you tell him/her?

If the intent here were "Did I tell him?," then it would be signed:

TELL   **FINISH**   **I**

Did I tell him/her?

Command forms rarely use pronouns:

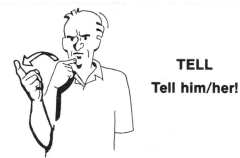

TELL

Tell him/her!

NEGATION

The most common way to negate a statement in ASL is to shake the head while you are making a sign. For example, to say "I do not understand," shake your head as you sign "I understand." The shaking of the head negates the statement so that it means "I do not understand." This practice applies to nearly all signs, including negative signs themselves. If the signer adds NOT in the above statement, and simultaneously shakes the head, the negation is emphasized. We know that English grammar does not permit double negatives, but in Spanish one may say "Yo no sé nada," which literally means "I not know nothing." Spanish here may be compared to ASL, where one may sign UNDERSTAND NOTHING while shaking the head, thus creating a double negative.

In general, a negative sign follows the thing it negates. It may also come before and it may come both before and after. For emphasis, however, it always follows the thing it negates. The latter is especially true in negative commands.

TELL ME   NONE   HE/SHE/IT

She tells me nothing.

TELL   NOT   I

I didn't tell him.

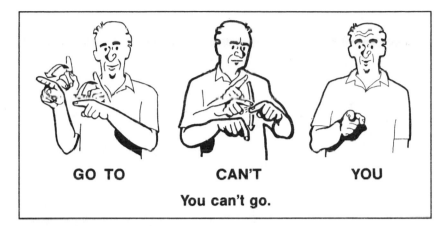

GO TO   **CAN'T**   **YOU**

You can't go.

Many signs have negation built into them:

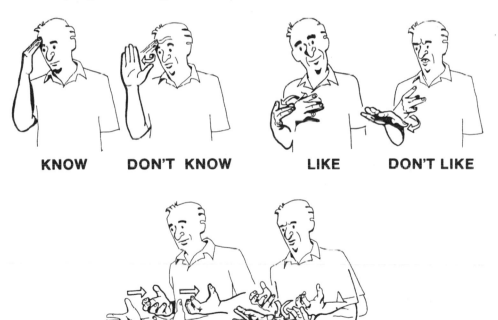

KNOW   DON'T KNOW   LIKE   DON'T LIKE

WANT   DON'T WANT

The signer should always shake the head while simultaneously making the negative form of the sign.

MORE FINAL SIGNS

In addition to the final position of the pronoun, there are other signs that tend to appear in the final position. For example,

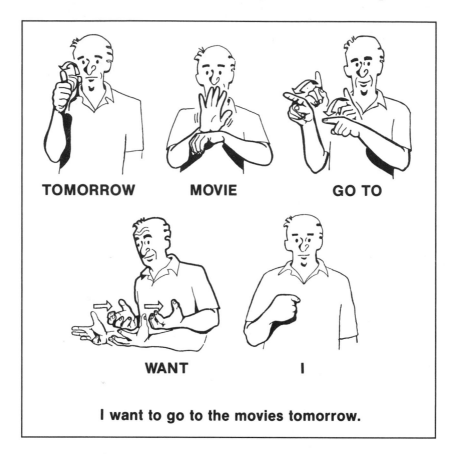

TOMORROW   MOVIE   GO TO

WANT   I

I want to go to the movies tomorrow.

The WANT sign comes after the verb because it belongs to a class of signs that expresses obligation, necessity, feelings, moods, states of mind, and intentions. Some other signs in this class are HOPE, CAN, MUST, and WILL. They do not always follow the verb, sometimes they precede it, and often they appear both before and after the verb.

NOW   AFTERNOON   CLEAR   HOPE

I hope it clears up this afternoon.

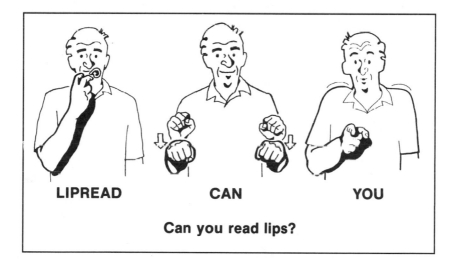

LIPREAD   CAN   YOU

Can you read lips?

The WILL sign is often confusing because it expresses both future tense and intention.

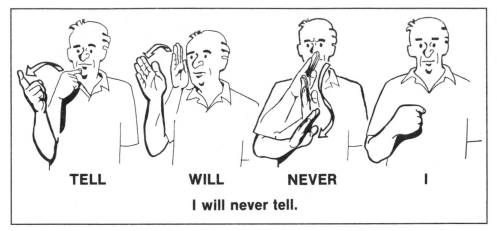

TELL   WILL   NEVER   I

I will never tell.

A final word about signs in the final position is that if you want to emphasize something, put it at or near the end of the statement. The last thing seen is the thing best remembered.

PLURALS

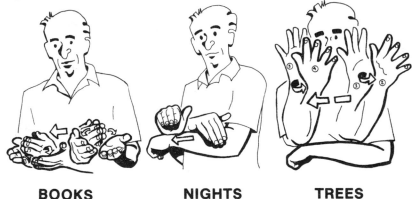

BOOKS   NIGHTS   TREES

Often signs are repeated or moved in a way that shows plurality.

When a sign does not lend itself to this kind of repetition or pluralizing movement, then signers use such signs as MANY, FEW, and SOME, or they use specific numbers such as NINE or FIFTY.

NAMES AND TITLES

When deaf people are talking to each other they rarely use each other's names. For example, "How are you, Bob?" becomes simply, "How you?" If, however, the signer asks the watcher about another person, then the signer uses that person's name. ("How is Bob?")

A person's name must be fingerspelled, but most deaf people also have name-signs. A name-sign is one that stands for that person, not for the name. Two people with the same name will have different name-signs. When you first meet a deaf person, you fingerspell your name. You tell him or her your name-sign only if he or she asks. Usually name-signs are not asked for until the relationship develops beyond that of a casual acquaintance.

Titles such as "Mrs.," "Dr.," and "Rev." are fingerspelled and used only when the person is being introduced. You never use them when you are talking directly to the person. "How are you, Dr. Smith?" becomes simply "How you?"

ARTICLES

There are no articles (a, an, the) in ASL.

A FINAL WORD

The acquisition of a spoken language involves principally learning grammar, pronunciation, and vocabulary. Except for pronunciation, the same applies to learning ASL. Forming signs clearly is the equivalent of pronunciation in ASL. Clarity in signing depends upon accuracy in making the sign, smoothness in execution of the sign, flow from one sign to the next without jerky or hesitant movements, the use of facial expressions, the use of head and body movements, and the proper use of space. The only way to develop these is through using the language with deaf people. They will correct you when you err, and by watching them carefully you will correct and fine-tune yourself.

3
Everyday Expressions

HELLO

Hello.

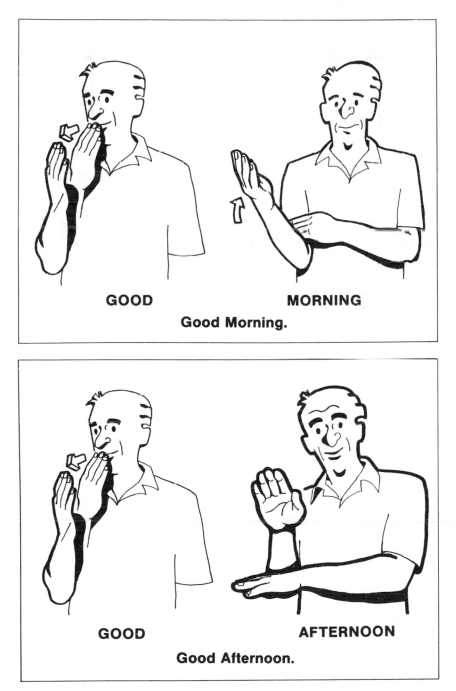

GOOD   **MORNING**

Good Morning.

GOOD   **AFTERNOON**

Good Afternoon.

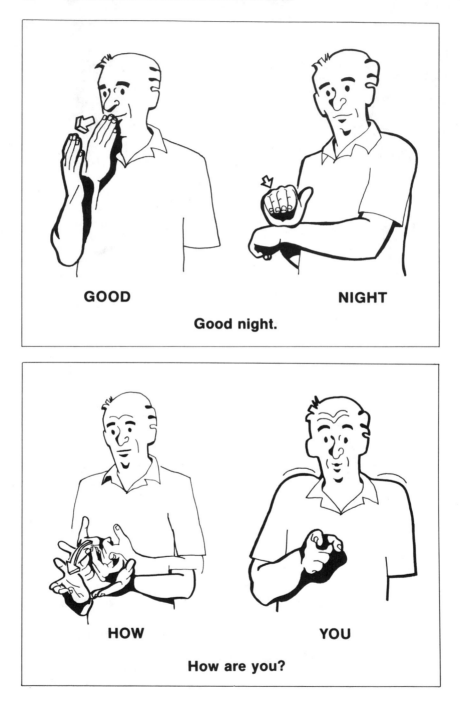

GOOD   **NIGHT**

Good night.

HOW   **YOU**

How are you?

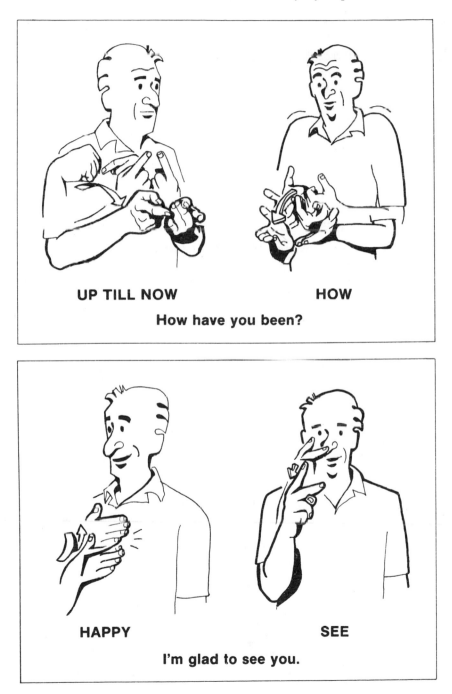

UP TILL NOW　　　　　**HOW**

How have you been?

HAPPY　　　　　**SEE**

I'm glad to see you.

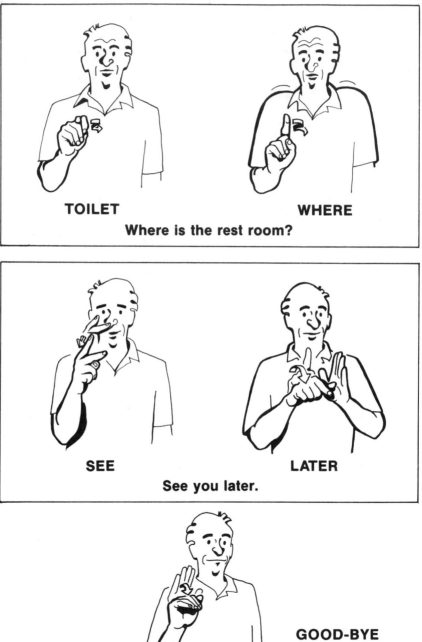

TOILET   **WHERE**

Where is the rest room?

SEE   **LATER**

See you later.

GOOD-BYE

Good-Bye.

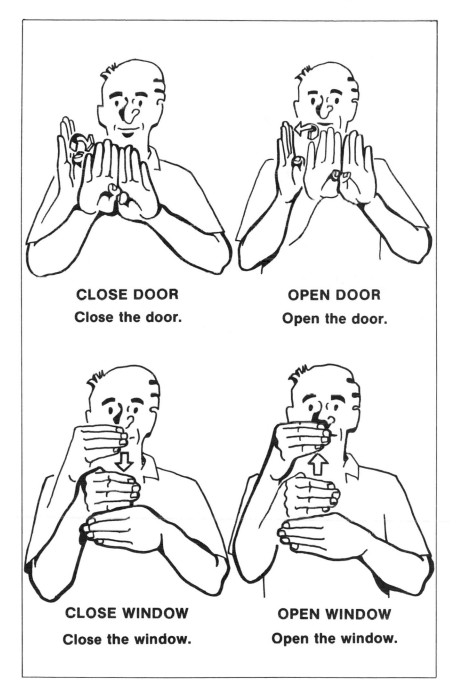

CLOSE DOOR
Close the door.

OPEN DOOR
Open the door.

CLOSE WINDOW
Close the window.

OPEN WINDOW
Open the window.

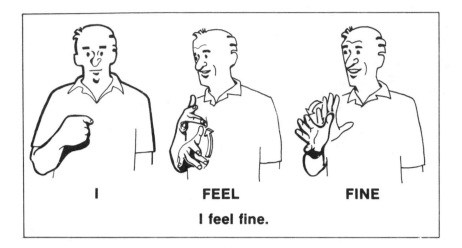

I   **FEEL**   **FINE**

I feel fine.

Additional vocabulary:

SICK

TIRED

LOUSY

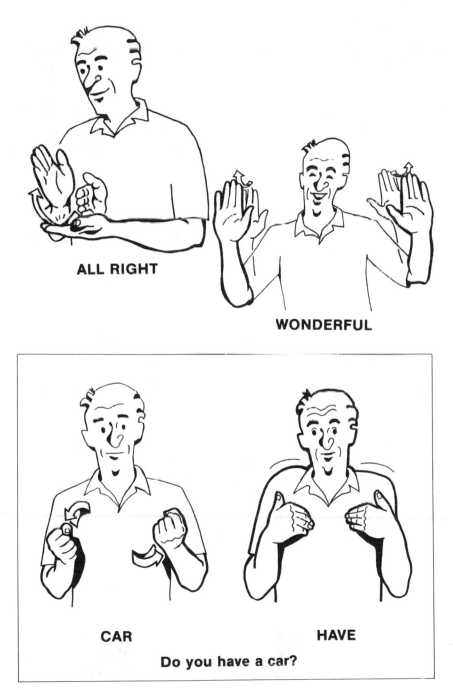

ALL RIGHT

WONDERFUL

CAR

HAVE

Do you have a car?

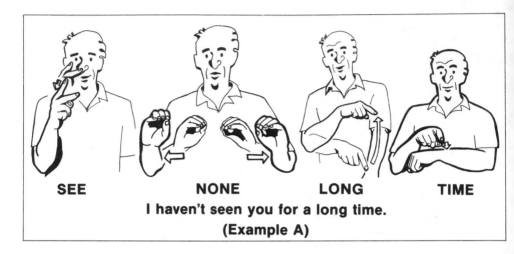

SEE   **NONE**   **LONG**   **TIME**

I haven't seen you for a long time.
(Example A)

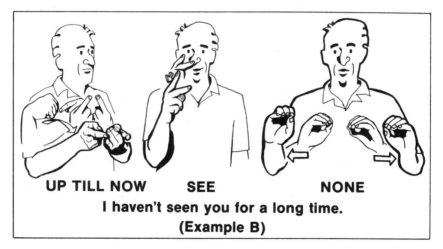

UP TILL NOW   **SEE**   **NONE**

I haven't seen you for a long time.
(Example B)

GOOD
Thank you.

PLEASE
Please.

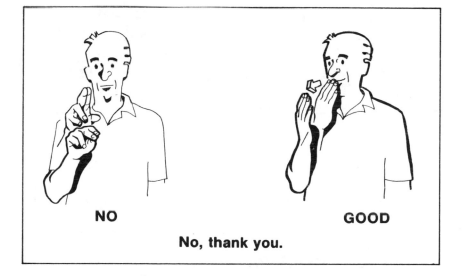

NO   **GOOD**

No, thank you.

EXCUSE
Pardon me.

T.V.   LOOK   LIKE

Do you like to watch T.V.?

MOVIE   GO TO   WANT

Do you want to go to the movies?

PHONE   **NUMBER**   **WHAT SHRUG**

What's your phone number?

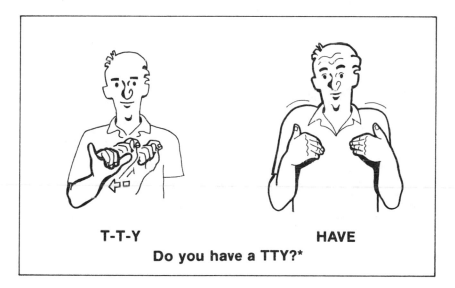

T-T-Y   **HAVE**

Do you have a TTY?*

---

*The TTY or TDD is a device that permits one to type messages back and forth over the telephone.

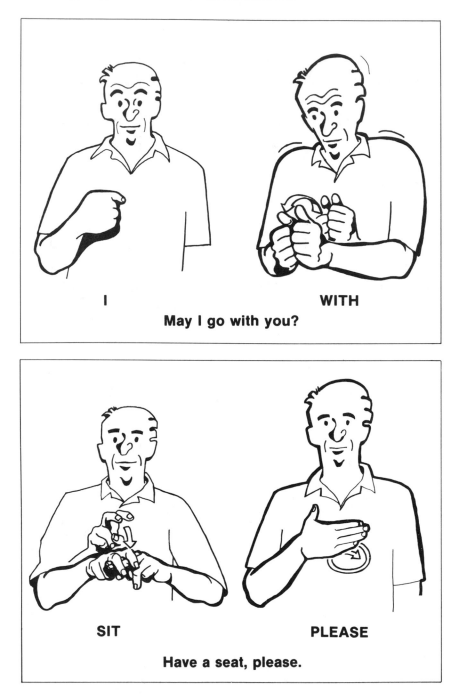

I

WITH

May I go with you?

SIT

PLEASE

Have a seat, please.

TIME

What time is it?

HOME   **GO**   **MUST**

I have to go home.

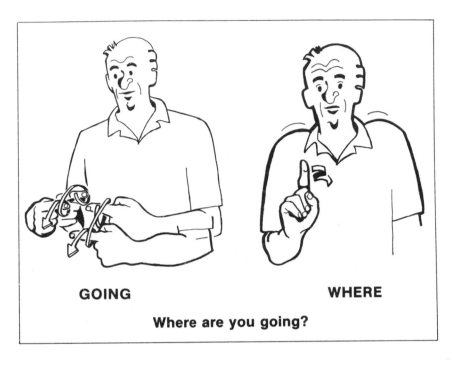

GOING   WHERE

Where are you going?

SORRY

I'm sorry.

4

Signing and Deafness

| I | LEARN | SIGN | LANGUAGE |

I'm learning sign language.

The sign LANGUAGE is usually not signed in this expression, so that it reads literally: "I am learning to sign."

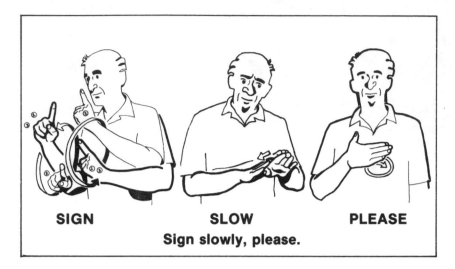

SIGN   **SLOW**   **PLEASE**

Sign slowly, please.

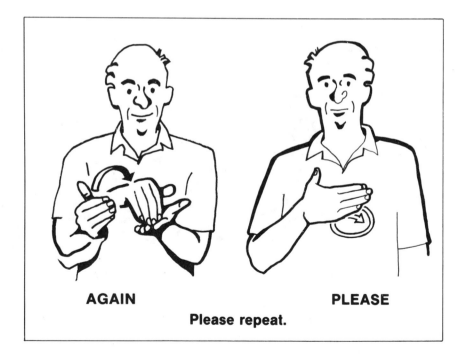

AGAIN   **PLEASE**

Please repeat.

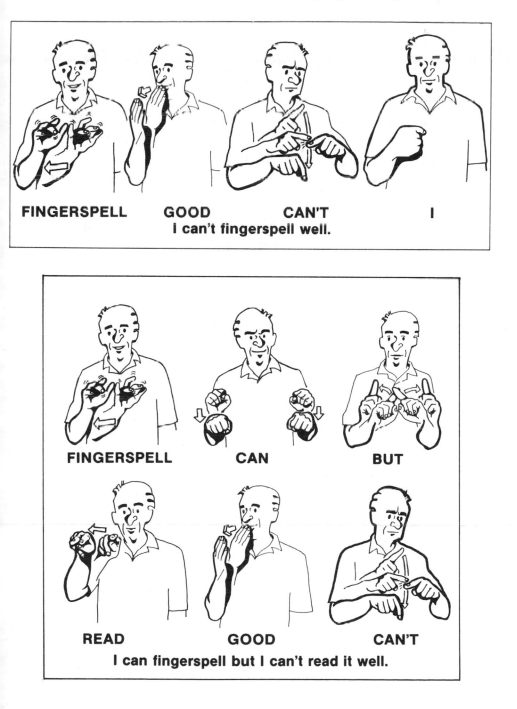

FINGERSPELL GOOD CAN'T I
I can't fingerspell well.

FINGERSPELL CAN BUT

READ GOOD CAN'T
I can fingerspell but I can't read it well.

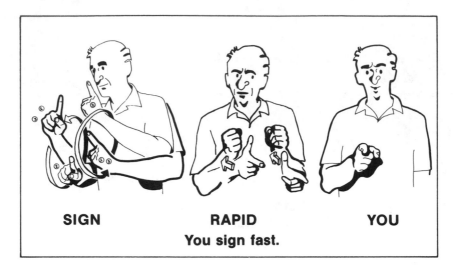

SIGN   **RAPID**   **YOU**
You sign fast.

UNDERSTAND
I don't understand.

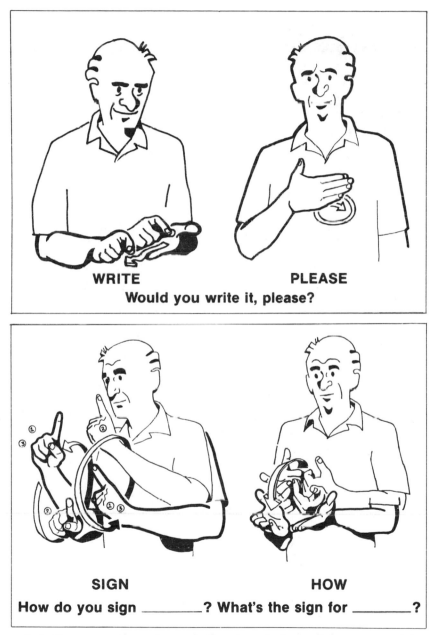

WRITE   **PLEASE**

Would you write it, please?

SIGN   **HOW**

How do you sign _____? What's the sign for _____?

Ask these questions by pointing to whatever it is you want to know the sign for or by fingerspelling the word.

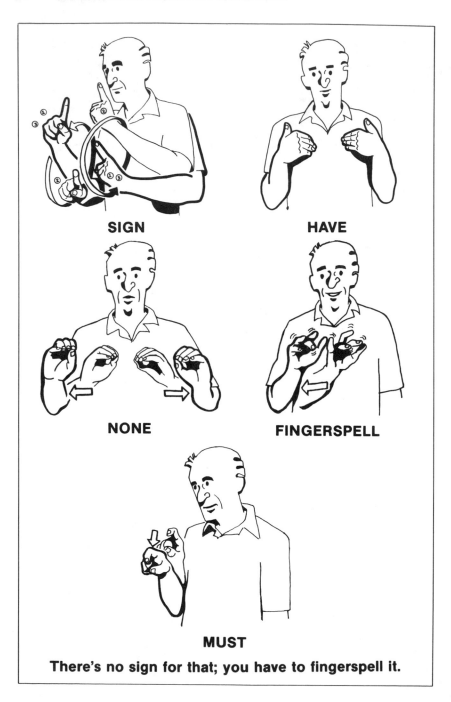

SIGN

HAVE

NONE

FINGERSPELL

MUST

There's no sign for that; you have to fingerspell it.

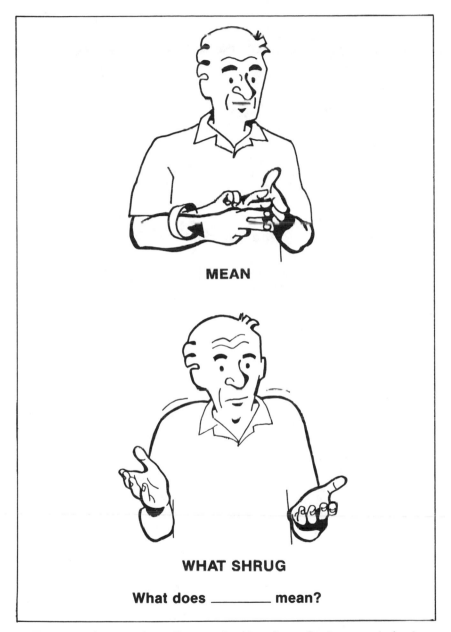

MEAN

WHAT SHRUG

What does _____ mean?

To ask this question, first make the sign of whatever it is that you want to know the meaning of, then sign MEAN WHAT SHRUG.

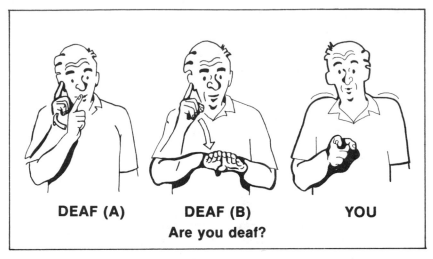

DEAF (A)   DEAF (B)   YOU
Are you deaf?

Either way of signing "deaf" is acceptable, but deaf people use the first one shown above more often than the second one.

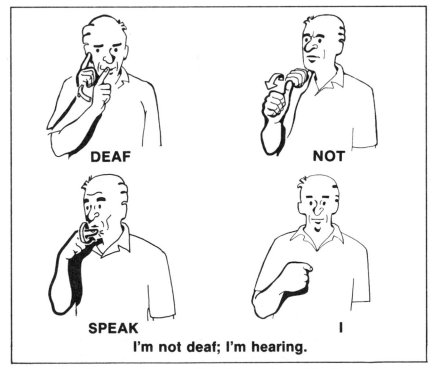

DEAF   NOT

SPEAK   I
I'm not deaf; I'm hearing.

Hearing people are referred to as "speaking" people.

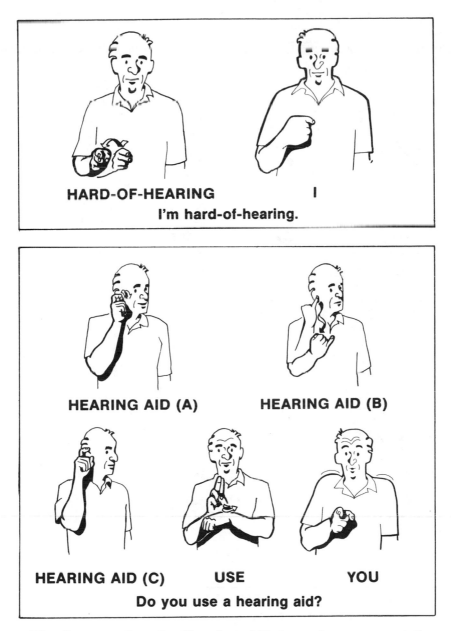

HARD-OF-HEARING   **I**
I'm hard-of-hearing.

HEARING AID (A)   **HEARING AID (B)**

HEARING AID (C)   USE   YOU
Do you use a hearing aid?

The first two signs for "hearing aid" shown here represent the kind of aid that is attached by a cord to a unit worn on the body. The third kind is the type worn behind the ear.

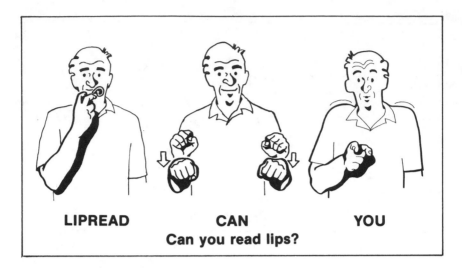

LIPREAD   **CAN**   **YOU**
Can you read lips?

SPEAK   **LITTLE BIT**
I speak a little.

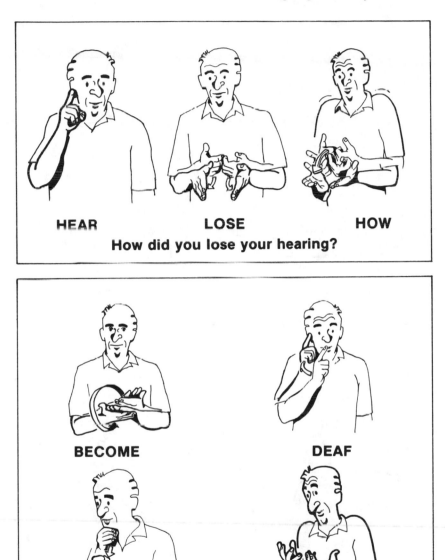

HEAR   **LOSE**   **HOW**

How did you lose your hearing?

BECOME   **DEAF**

OLD   **HOW MANY**

How old were you when you became deaf?

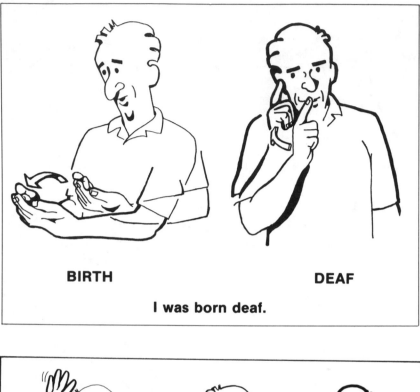

BIRTH   **DEAF**

I was born deaf.

FATHER   **MOTHER**   **DEAF**

Are your parents deaf?

C-L-U-B

VISIT   **WANT**   **I**

I want to visit the club for deaf people.

Fingerspell "C-L-U-B" at the beginning of this sentence. It is not necessary to sign "for deaf people", because the word "club" implies that.

T.V.   **SENTENCE**   **PLEASE**   **I**

I enjoy watching T.V. with captions.

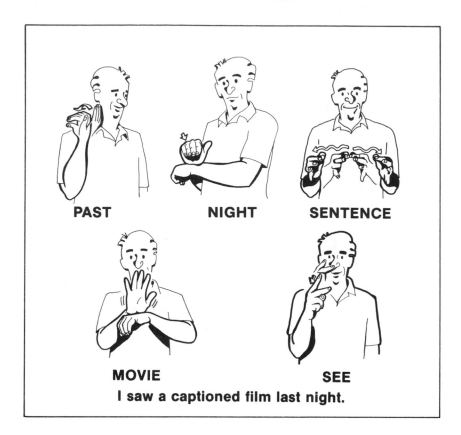

PAST   NIGHT   SENTENCE

MOVIE   SEE

I saw a captioned film last night.

INSTITUTE   GO TO   PAST   YOU

Did you go to a residential school for deaf children?

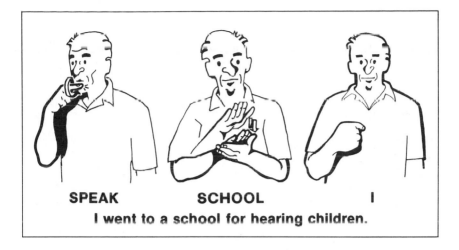

SPEAK   SCHOOL   I

I went to a school for hearing children.

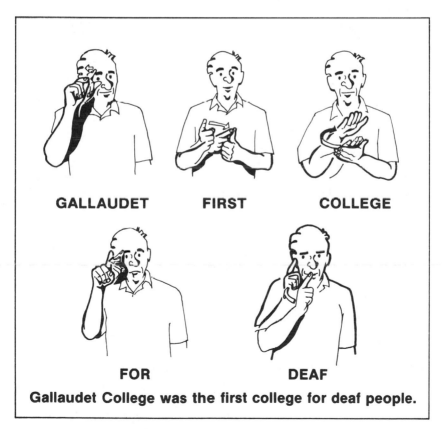

GALLAUDET   FIRST   COLLEGE

FOR   DEAF

Gallaudet College was the first college for deaf people.

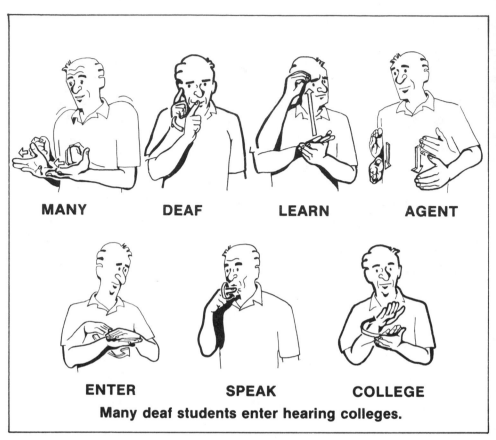

MANY   DEAF   LEARN   AGENT

ENTER   SPEAK   COLLEGE

Many deaf students enter hearing colleges.

Sometimes "D-C" is fingerspelled after the sign for "Washington."

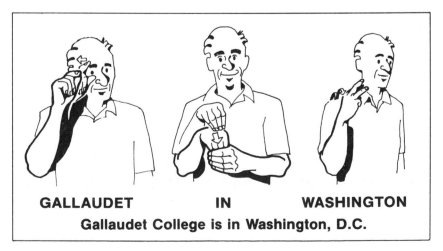

GALLAUDET   IN   WASHINGTON

Gallaudet College is in Washington, D.C.

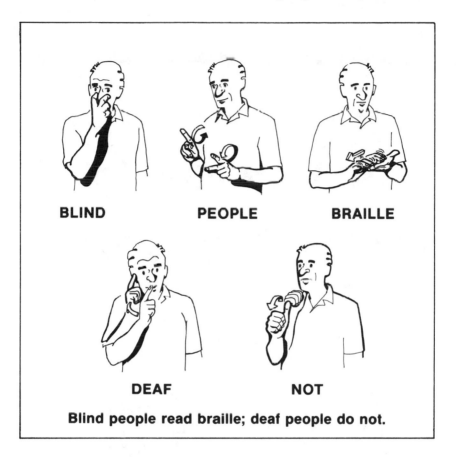

BLIND   **PEOPLE**   **BRAILLE**

DEAF   **NOT**

Blind people read braille; deaf people do not.

5

Getting Acquainted

NAME   WHAT SHRUG

What is your name?

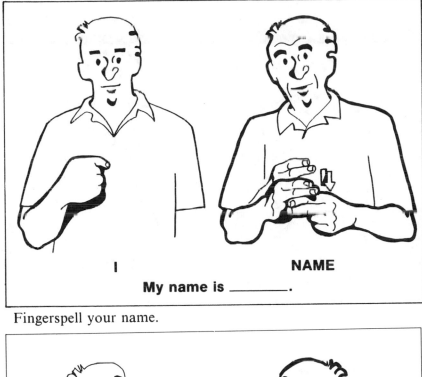

I

NAME

My name is _____.

Fingerspell your name.

HAPPY

MEET

I'm happy to meet you.

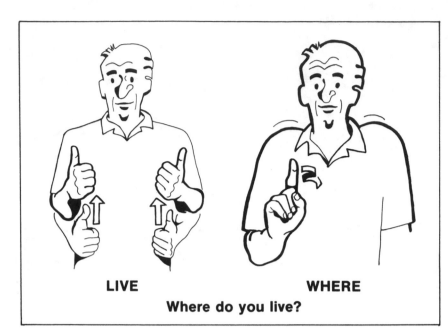

LIVE   **WHERE**

Where do you live?

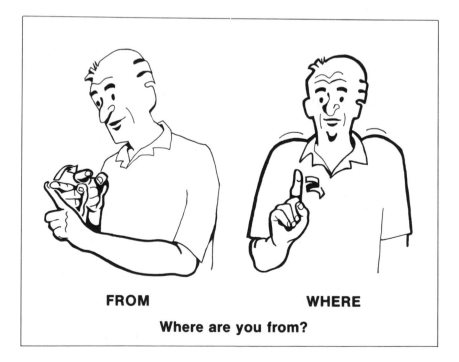

FROM   **WHERE**

Where are you from?

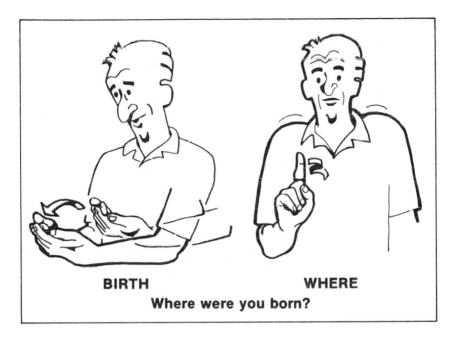

BIRTH   **WHERE**
Where were you born?

INTRODUCE   **WIFE**
May I introduce my wife?

After making the sign for the person you are introducing, you then fingerspell that person's name.

Additional vocabulary:

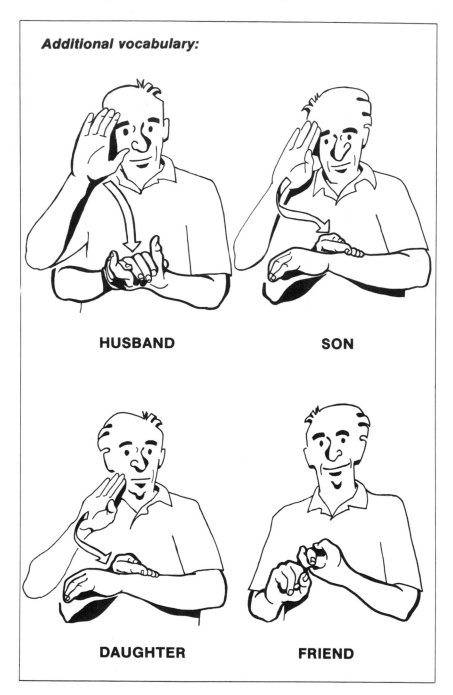

HUSBAND

SON

DAUGHTER

FRIEND

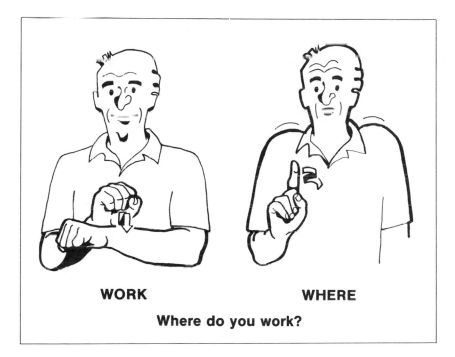

WORK   **WHERE**

Where do you work?

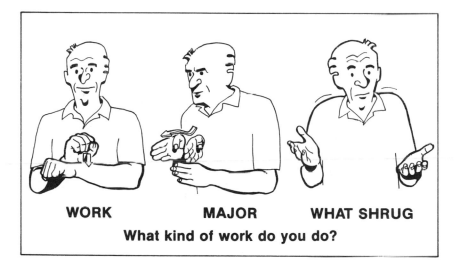

WORK   **MAJOR**   **WHAT SHRUG**

What kind of work do you do?

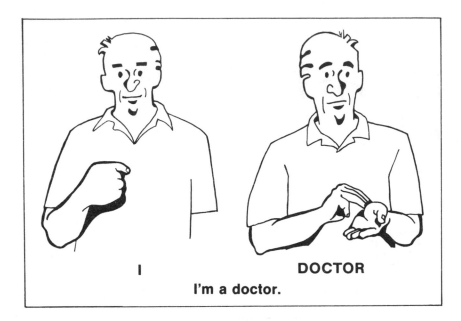

I   DOCTOR

I'm a doctor.

Additional vocabulary:

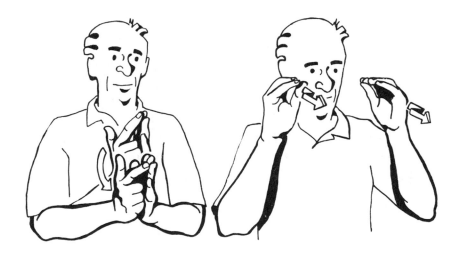

LAW   TEACH

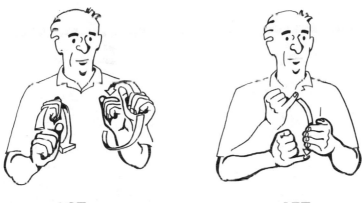

ACT   **ART**

The AGENT sign is often added to a verb or noun sign to indicate that one does or is what the verb or noun sign says. Here the AGENT sign could be added to TEACH, LAW, ACT, and ART, but would not be added to DOCTOR, POLICE, HOUSE-WIFE, FIREFIGHTER, or SECRETARY. The use of the AGENT sign is optional.

AGENT   **FIREFIGHTER**

POLICE   **SECRETARY**

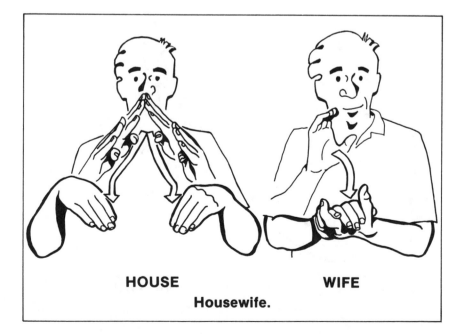

HOUSE   **WIFE**

Housewife.

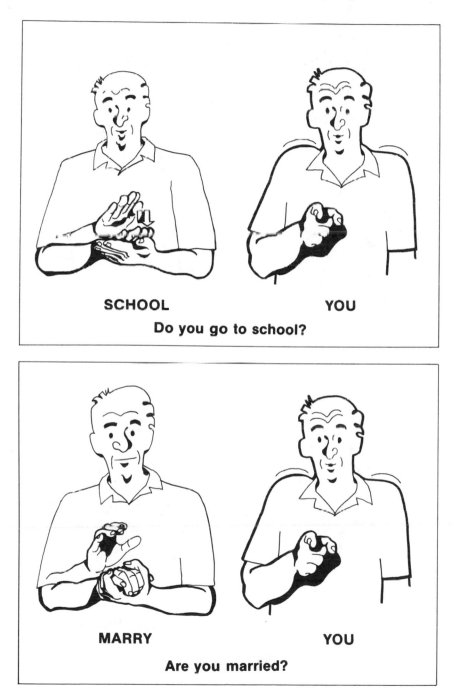

SCHOOL   **YOU**

Do you go to school?

MARRY   **YOU**

Are you married?

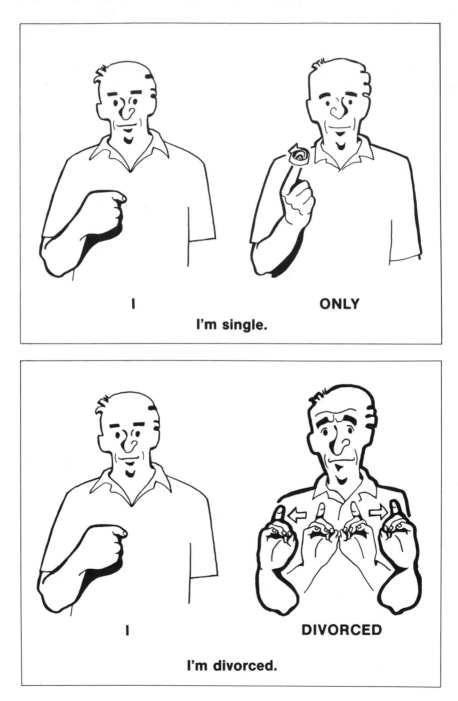

I   ONLY

I'm single.

I   DIVORCED

I'm divorced.

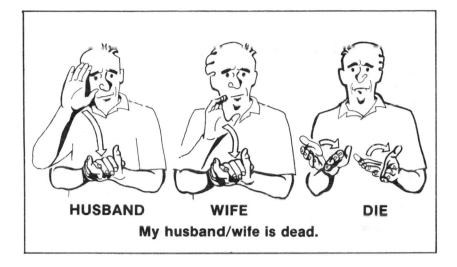

HUSBAND   **WIFE**   **DIE**

My husband/wife is dead.

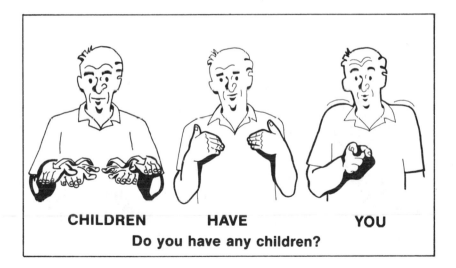

CHILDREN   **HAVE**   **YOU**

Do you have any children?

CHILDREN   HAVE   HOW MANY

How many children do you have?

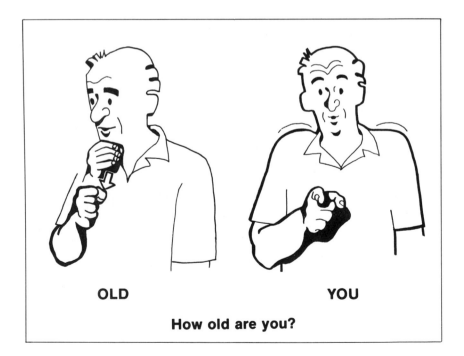

OLD   YOU

How old are you?

SMOKE CIGARETTE   **COMPLAIN**

Do you mind if I smoke?

ALL RIGHT
It's all right. It's okay.

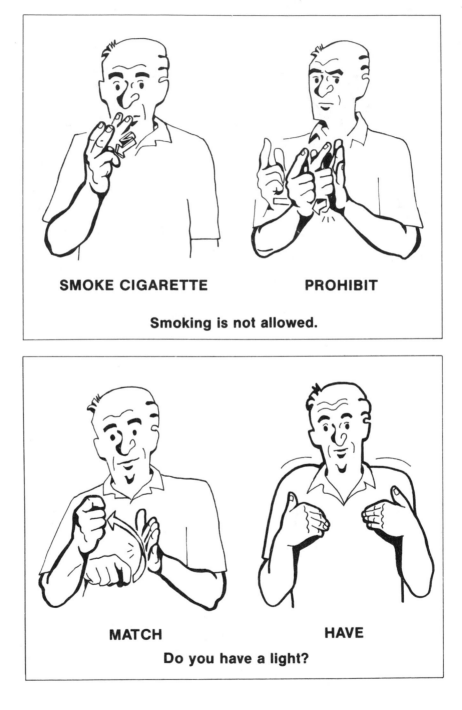

SMOKE CIGARETTE   **PROHIBIT**

Smoking is not allowed.

MATCH   **HAVE**

Do you have a light?

6

Health

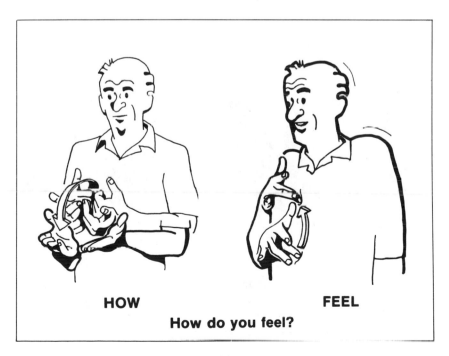

HOW   FEEL

How do you feel?

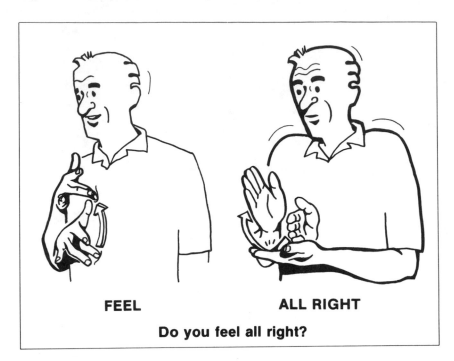

FEEL   **ALL RIGHT**

Do you feel all right?

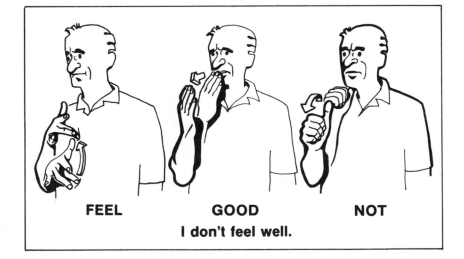

FEEL   GOOD   NOT

I don't feel well.

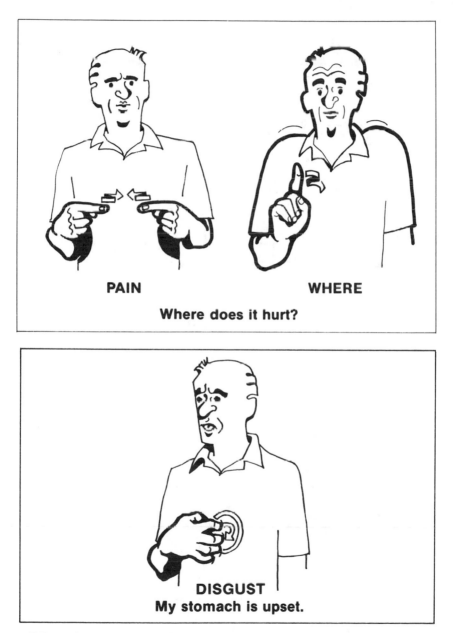

PAIN   **WHERE**

Where does it hurt?

DISGUST
My stomach is upset.

When done alone, as it is done here, this sign may also mean that something is disgusting. Context determines which meaning is intended.

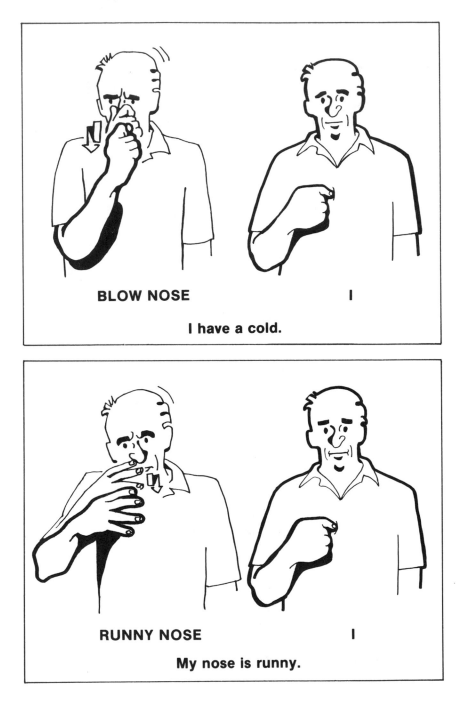

BLOW NOSE   I

I have a cold.

RUNNY NOSE   I

My nose is runny.

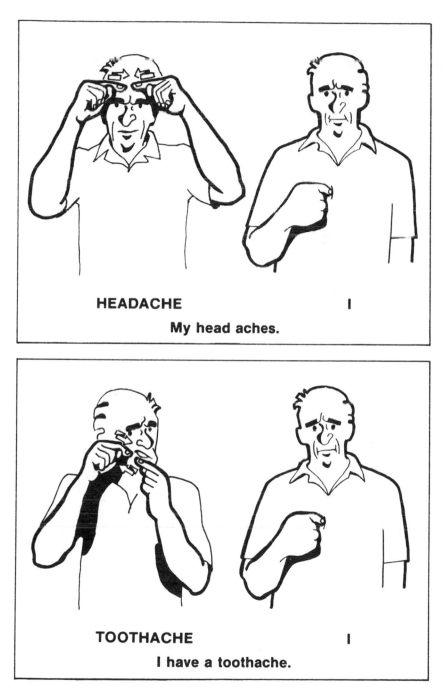

HEADACHE   **I**

My head aches.

TOOTHACHE   **I**

I have a toothache.

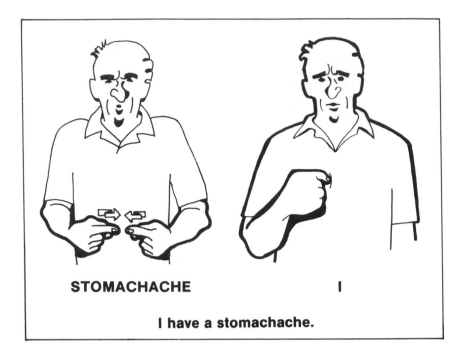

STOMACHACHE   **I**

I have a stomachache.

The sign PAIN may be placed anywhere on the body to denote that you are hurt or have a pain in that part of the body.

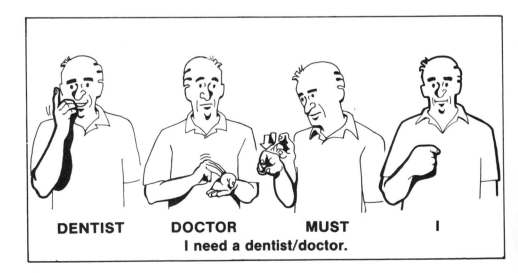

DENTIST   **DOCTOR**   **MUST**   **I**

I need a dentist/doctor.

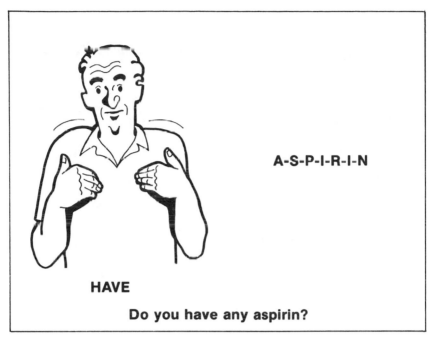

A-S-P-I-R-I-N

HAVE

Do you have any aspirin?

Fingerspell ASPIRIN.

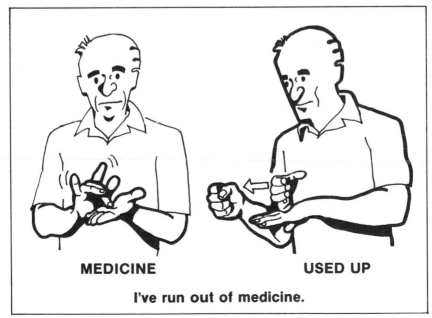

MEDICINE   **USED UP**

I've run out of medicine.

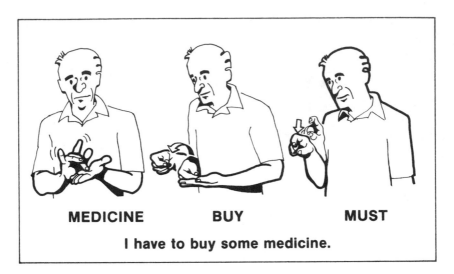

MEDICINE   **BUY**   **MUST**

I have to buy some medicine.

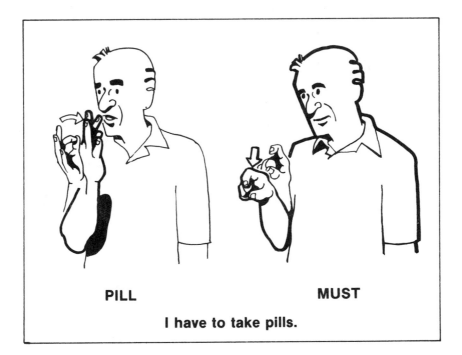

PILL   **MUST**

I have to take pills.

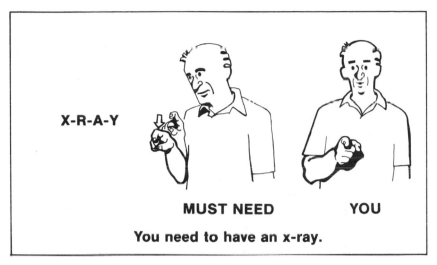

X-R-A-Y

MUST NEED   **YOU**

You need to have an x-ray.

Fingerspell X-RAY.

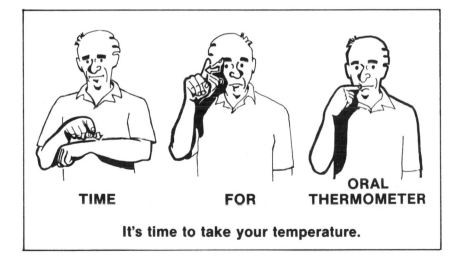

TIME   **FOR**   **ORAL THERMOMETER**

It's time to take your temperature.

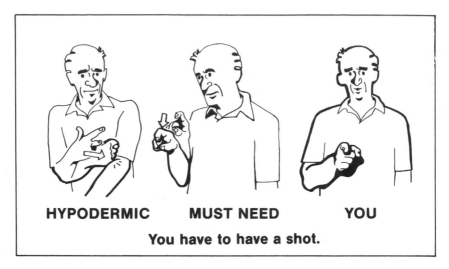

HYPODERMIC   MUST NEED   YOU

You have to have a shot.

The MUST sign may mean "need" or "should" and is done differently depending upon the meaning desired. If something is mandatory, then make one movement down. If something is optional but desirable, then make two gentle downward movements.

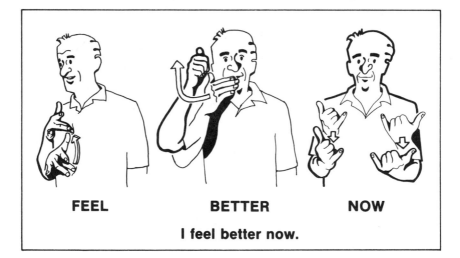

FEEL   BETTER   NOW

I feel better now.

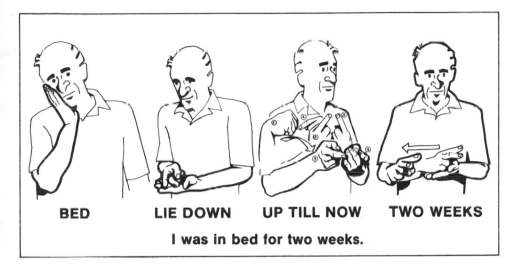

BED　　**LIE DOWN**　　**UP TILL NOW**　　**TWO WEEKS**

I was in bed for two weeks.

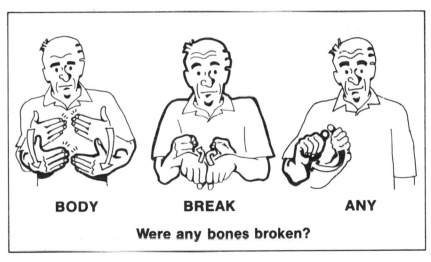

BODY　　**BREAK**　　**ANY**

Were any bones broken?

There is no standard sign for "bone," so the statement here is more generally read as, "Is anything in your body broken?" If you wish to sign "bone" specifically, then you must fingerspell it or find out what the local sign for it is.

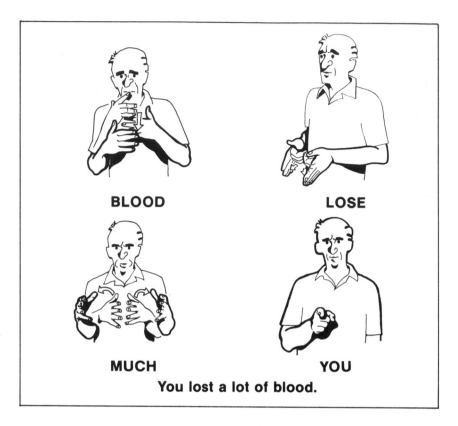

BLOOD

LOSE

MUCH

YOU

You lost a lot of blood.

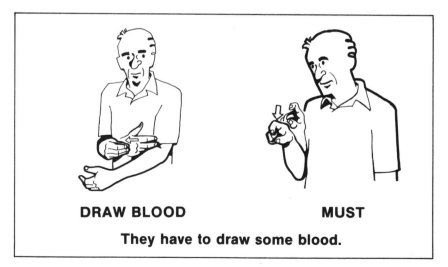

DRAW BLOOD

MUST

They have to draw some blood.

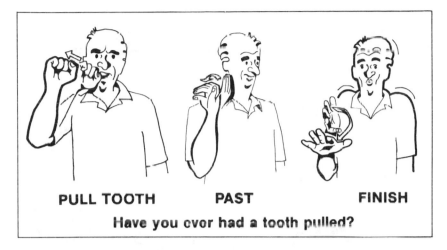

PULL TOOTH   **PAST**   **FINISH**

Have you ever had a tooth pulled?

The signs PAST and FINISH both refer to the past. Either one may be used alone here, but it is very common to see them both appear in a statement.

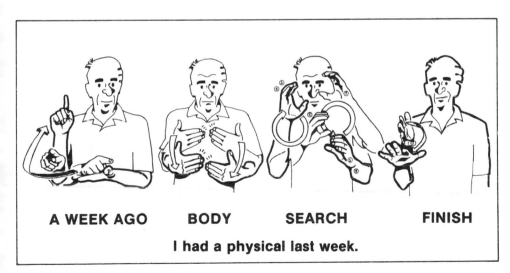

A WEEK AGO   **BODY**   **SEARCH**   **FINISH**

I had a physical last week.

The use of the FINISH sign here denotes the idea that I "already" had a physical last week.

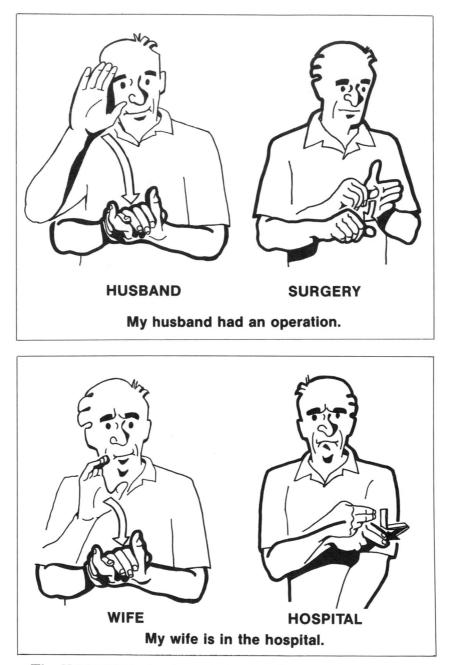

HUSBAND   **SURGERY**

My husband had an operation.

WIFE   **HOSPITAL**

My wife is in the hospital.

The HOSPITAL sign is made by drawing a cross on the sleeve.

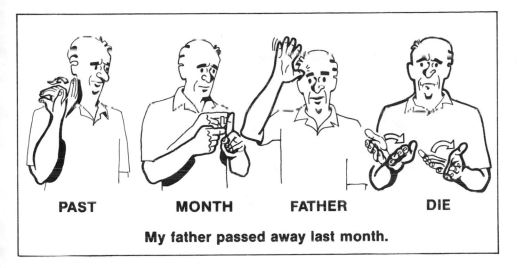

PAST   MONTH   FATHER   DIE

My father passed away last month.

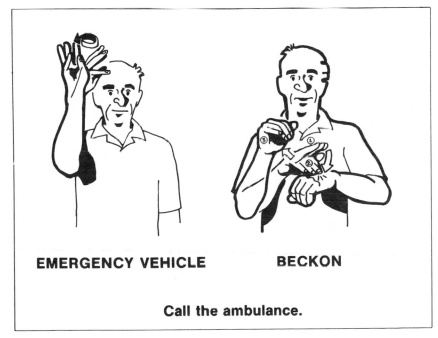

EMERGENCY VEHICLE   BECKON

Call the ambulance.

The sign for "ambulance" indicates the spinning red light on top of the vehicle and may refer to any emergency vehicle or just the flashing red light itself. Also, instead of the sign BECKON, you may sign PHONE.

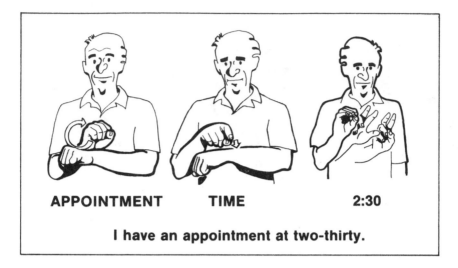

APPOINTMENT   **TIME**   **2:30**

I have an appointment at two-thirty.

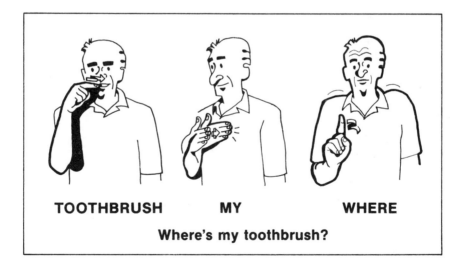

TOOTHBRUSH   **MY**   **WHERE**

Where's my toothbrush?

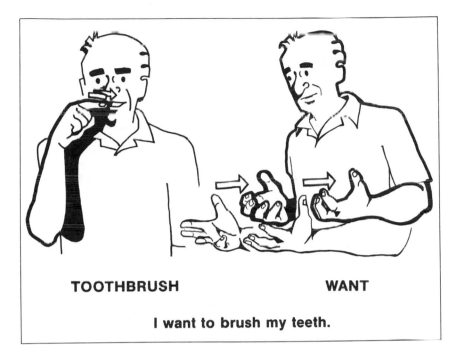

TOOTHBRUSH   **WANT**

I want to brush my teeth.

BATH   **SHOWER**   **FINISH**

I already took a bath/shower.

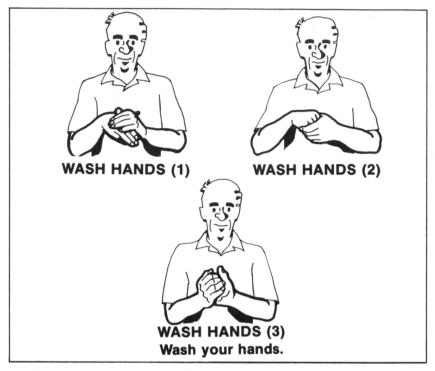

WASH HANDS (1)   **WASH HANDS (2)**

WASH HANDS (3)
Wash your hands.

The above sign, shown in three steps, is a mime of actually washing the hands, as the sign below is a mime of actually washing the face.

WASH FACE
Wash your face.

SHAVE

LATE

I haven't shaved yet.

HAIR DRYER

LEND

May I borrow your hair dryer?

BRUSH HAIR
Brush your hair.

COMB   LOSE

I lost my comb.

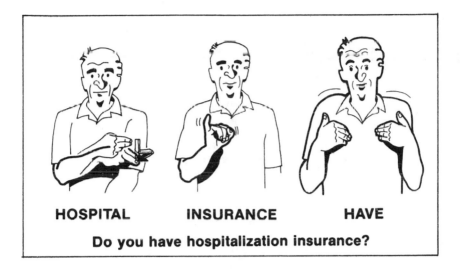

HOSPITAL   **INSURANCE**   **HAVE**

Do you have hospitalization insurance?

7
Weather

NOW   DAY   PRETTY

It's beautiful today.

SUN   **HOT**

The sun is hot.

SIT   **SUNRAY**   **PLEASE**

I enjoy sitting in the sun.

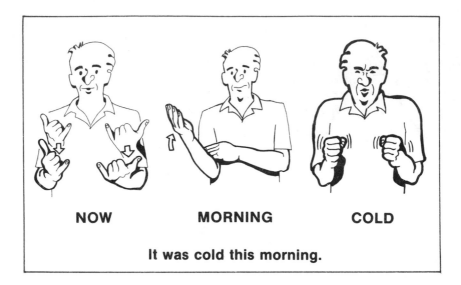

NOW   **MORNING**   **COLD**

It was cold this morning.

NOW   **NIGHT**   **ICE**

It will freeze tonight.

TOMORROW **SNOW** **MAYBE**

Maybe it will snow tomorrow.

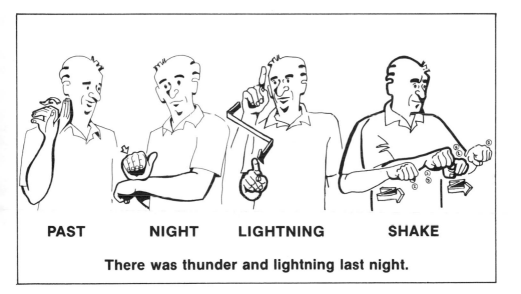

PAST **NIGHT** **LIGHTNING** **SHAKE**

There was thunder and lightning last night.

YESTERDAY   **RAIN**

It rained yesterday.

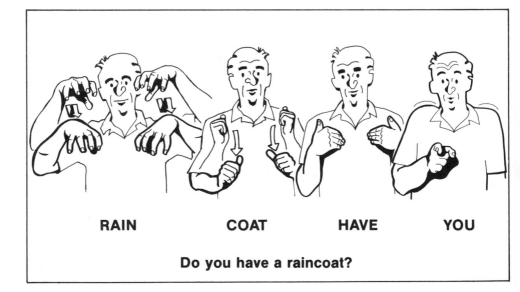

RAIN   **COAT**   **HAVE**   **YOU**

Do you have a raincoat?

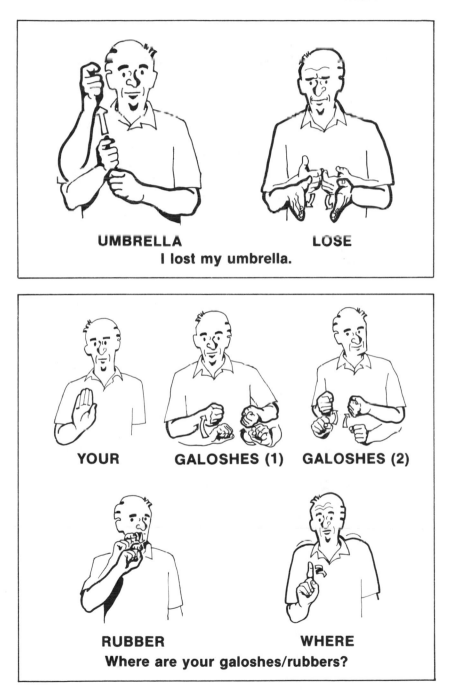

UMBRELLA   **LOSE**
I lost my umbrella.

YOUR   **GALOSHES (1)**   **GALOSHES (2)**

RUBBER   **WHERE**
Where are your galoshes/rubbers?

NOW   DAY   WIND (1)   WIND (2)

It's windy today.

YESTERDAY   LATE AFTERNOON   SUNSET

CLOUDS   PRETTY

Yesterday evening at sunset, the clouds were beautiful.

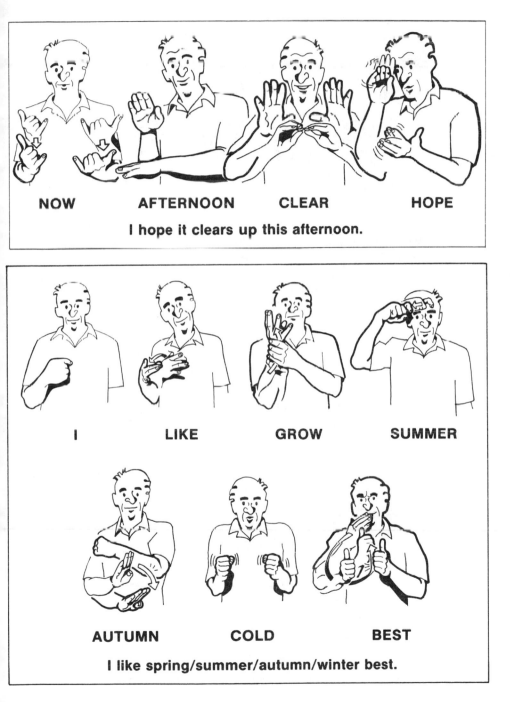

NOW   **AFTERNOON**   **CLEAR**   **HOPE**

I hope it clears up this afternoon.

I   **LIKE**   **GROW**   **SUMMER**

AUTUMN   **COLD**   **BEST**

I like spring/summer/autumn/winter best.

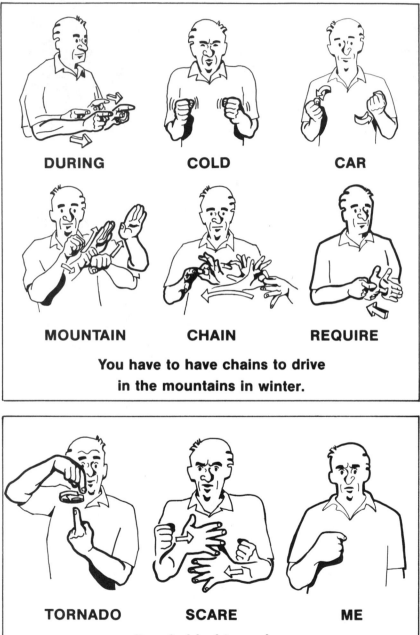

DURING   **COLD**   **CAR**

MOUNTAIN   **CHAIN**   **REQUIRE**

**You have to have chains to drive
in the mountains in winter.**

TORNADO   **SCARE**   **ME**

I'm afraid of tornados.

TEMPERATURE   **WHAT SHRUG**

What's the temperature?

SNOW   **MELT**   **FINISH**

Has the snow melted?

LAST YEAR   **WATER**   **FLOOD**

There was a flood last year.

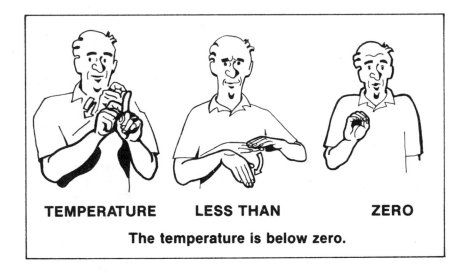

TEMPERATURE   **LESS THAN**   **ZERO**

The temperature is below zero.

EARTH   **SHAKE**

FINISH   **YOU**

Have you ever been in an earthquake?

There are no signs for "hurricane," "blizzard," "sleet," and "hail," so they must be fingerspelled.

8
Family

| YOUR | FATHER | FACE | NICE |

Your father is nice looking.

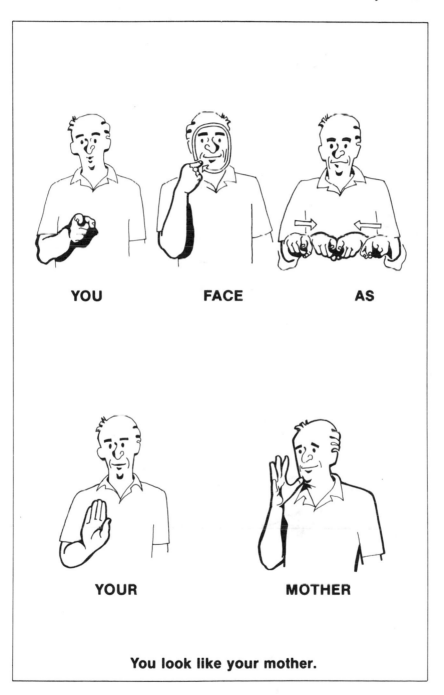

YOU   FACE   AS

YOUR   MOTHER

You look like your mother.

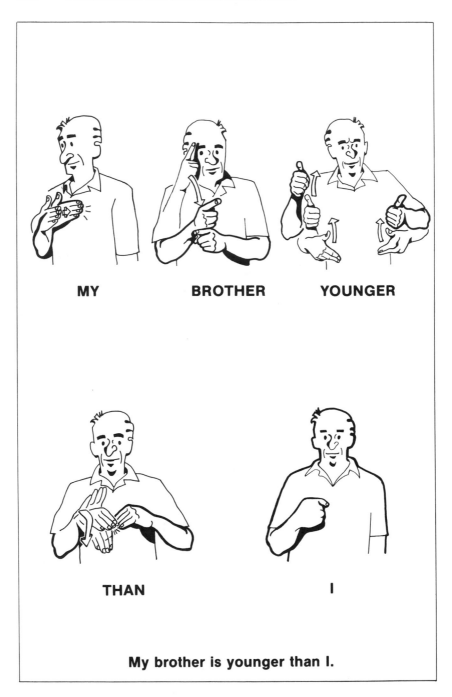

My brother is younger than I.

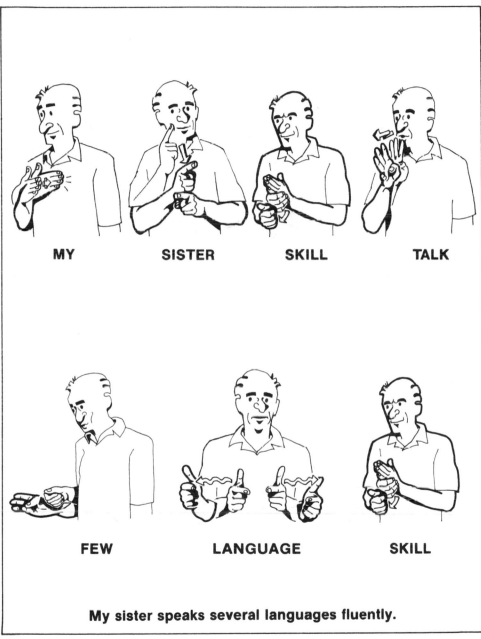

MY   SISTER   SKILL   TALK

FEW   LANGUAGE   SKILL

My sister speaks several languages fluently.

The repetition of a sign, as SKILL is repeated here, is a common practice.

HIS/HER/ITS   **SON**   **AIM**

ROCKET   **AGENT**

His son wants to be an astronaut.

| HIS/HER/ITS | DAUGHTER | WORK | HERE |

Her daughter works here.

| MY | UNCLE | FARM | AGENT |

My uncle is a farmer.

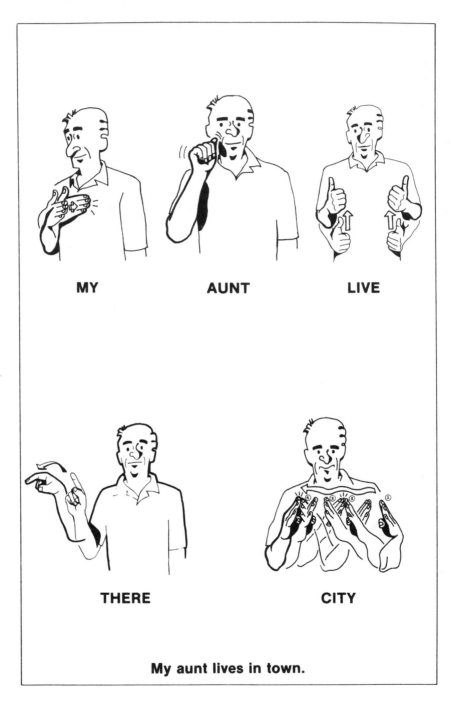

MY   **AUNT**   **LIVE**

THERE   **CITY**

My aunt lives in town.

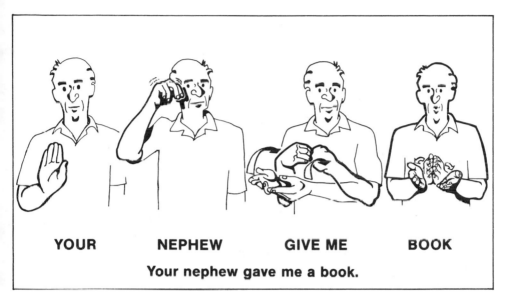

YOUR   **NEPHEW**   **GIVE ME**   **BOOK**

Your nephew gave me a book.

HIS/HER/ITS   **NIECE**   **SHE HELP YOU**   **WILL**

His niece will help you.

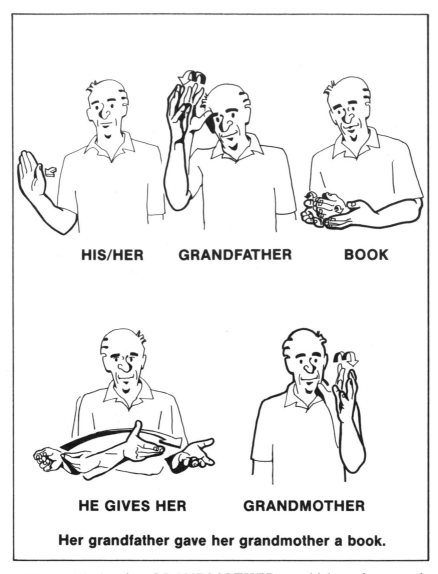

HIS/HER   GRANDFATHER   BOOK

HE GIVES HER   GRANDMOTHER

Her grandfather gave her grandmother a book.

Normally the sign GRANDMOTHER would have been made with the right hand, but since the action of the GIVE sign moves from the signer's right to the signer's left, making the GRANDMOTHER sign with the left hand makes it visually clearer who is on which side. (For further explanation, see page 20, "Placement of Signs.")

MY

COUSIN

AIRPLANE

AGENT

My cousin is a pilot.

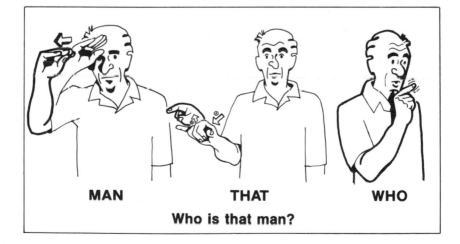

MAN

THAT

WHO

Who is that man?

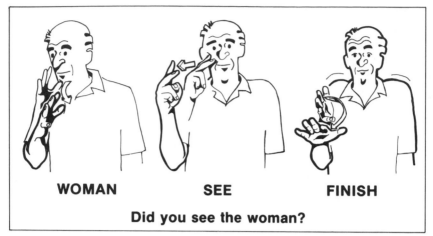

WOMAN   **SEE**   **FINISH**

Did you see the woman?

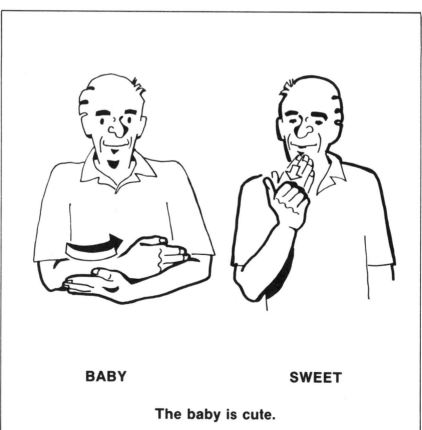

BABY   **SWEET**

The baby is cute.

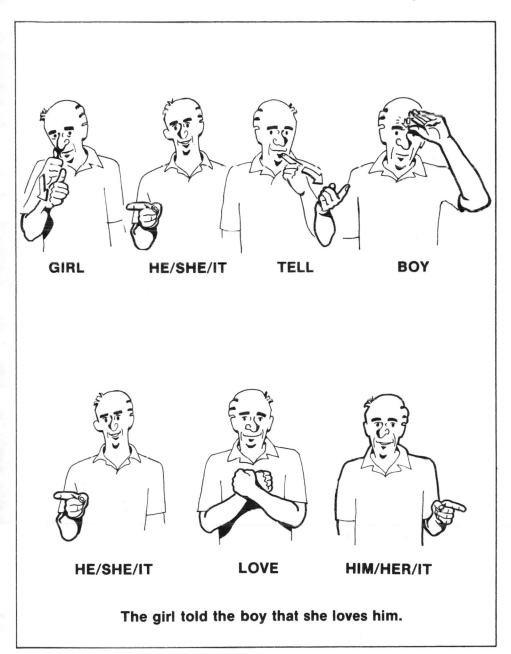

GIRL   HE/SHE/IT   TELL   BOY

HE/SHE/IT   LOVE   HIM/HER/IT

The girl told the boy that she loves him.

The use of both hands in making the sign helps reinforce visually who is doing what to whom.

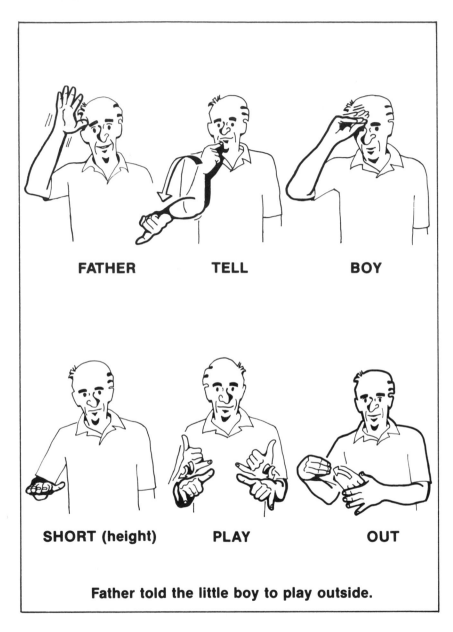

FATHER   TELL   BOY

SHORT (height)   PLAY   OUT

Father told the little boy to play outside.

The TELL sign moves downward to denote that the person being told is a child. The same thing occurs in the following sentence with the HER sign.

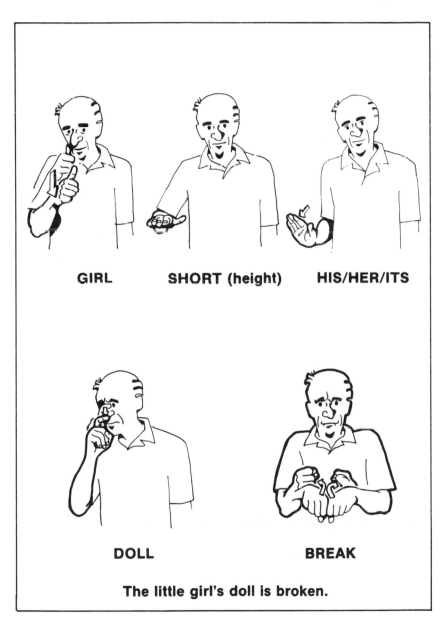

GIRL   SHORT (height)   HIS/HER/ITS

DOLL   BREAK

The little girl's doll is broken.

CHILDREN   **COME HERE**   **HOW MANY**

How many children are coming?

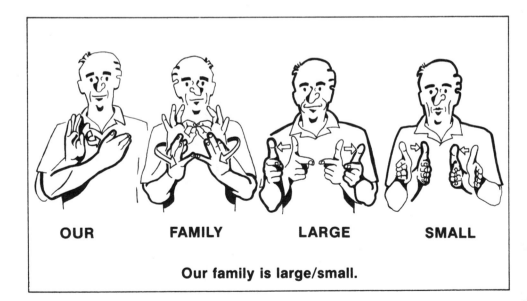

OUR   **FAMILY**   **LARGE**   **SMALL**

Our family is large/small.

PAST   SUMMER   FAMILY   CONVENE

We had a family reunion last summer.

The idea "we had" is understood and therefore not signed.

WE   CONVENE   GRANDFATHER

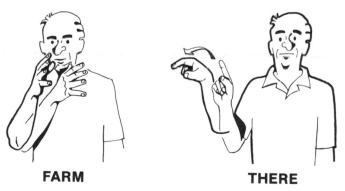

FARM   THERE

We met at Grandfather's farm.

9
School

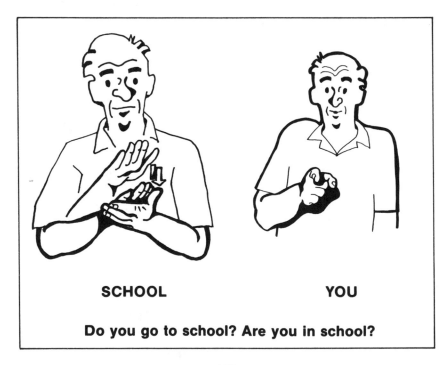

SCHOOL

YOU

Do you go to school? Are you in school?

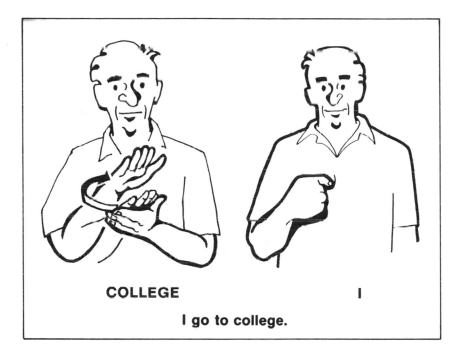

COLLEGE   **I**

I go to college.

I   **MAJOR**   **ENGLISH**

I'm majoring in English.

Additional vocabulary:

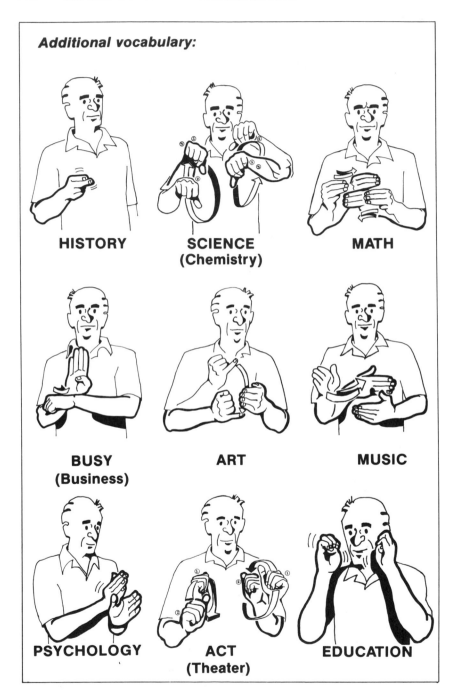

HISTORY

SCIENCE
(Chemistry)

MATH

BUSY
(Business)

ART

MUSIC

PSYCHOLOGY

ACT
(Theater)

EDUCATION

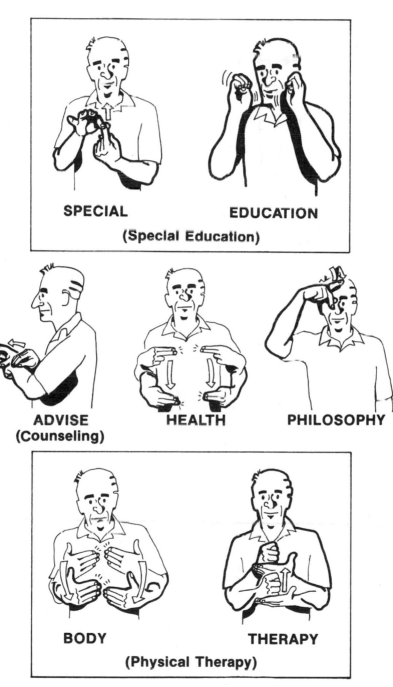

SPECIAL   **EDUCATION**

(Special Education)

ADVISE   **HEALTH**   **PHILOSOPHY**
(Counseling)

BODY   **THERAPY**

(Physical Therapy)

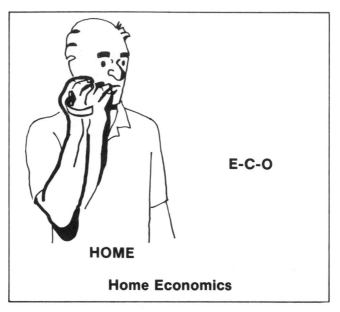

E-C-O

HOME

Home Economics

"Home Economics" is expressed by first signing HOME and then fingerspelling E-C-O.

COMPUTER

The sign for "computer" varies a good deal around the country, so check it out with your local deaf people.

Other academic fields are fingerspelled, either in full or in abbreviated form. "Physical Education" is "P–E;" "Library Science" is "L-S;" "Sociology" is "S-O-C," and so on.

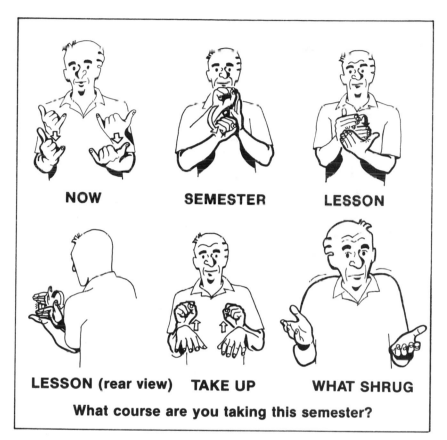

NOW   **SEMESTER**   **LESSON**

LESSON (rear view)   **TAKE UP**   **WHAT SHRUG**

What course are you taking this semester?

LEARN   **AGENT**   I

I'm a student.

Additional vocabulary:

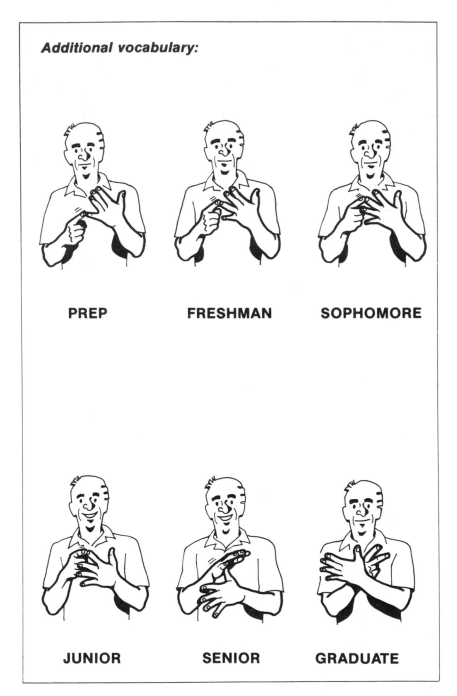

PREP   FRESHMAN   SOPHOMORE

JUNIOR   SENIOR   GRADUATE

LAST YEAR   **GRADUATE**   **I**

I graduated last year.

NOW   **GRADUATE**   **SCHOOL**   **I**

I'm in graduate school now.

STUDY   **LIKE**   **I**

I like to study.

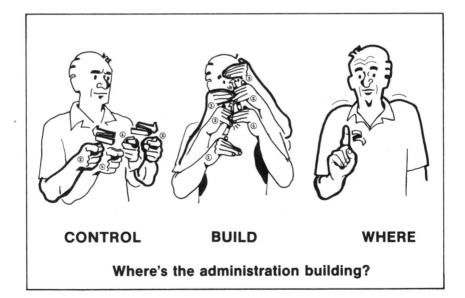

CONTROL   **BUILD**   **WHERE**

Where's the administration building?

LIBRARY   **GO TO**   **RESEARCH**   **MUST**

You've got to go to the library and do some research.

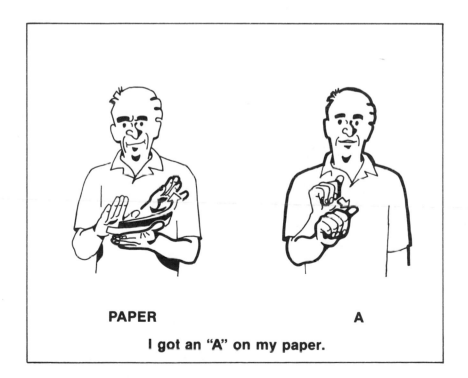

PAPER   **A**

I got an "A" on my paper.

STUDY   ALL NIGHT

I studied all night.

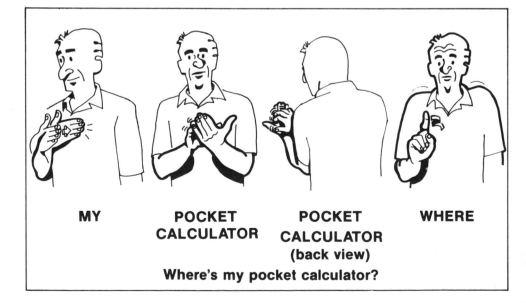

MY   POCKET   POCKET   WHERE
            CALCULATOR   CALCULATOR
                            (back view)

Where's my pocket calculator?

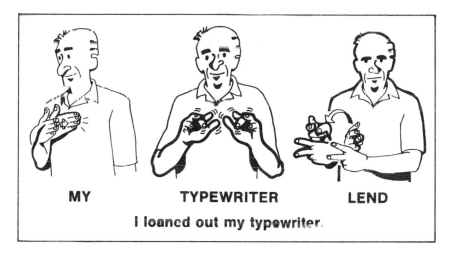

MY **TYPEWRITER** **LEND**

I loaned out my typewriter.

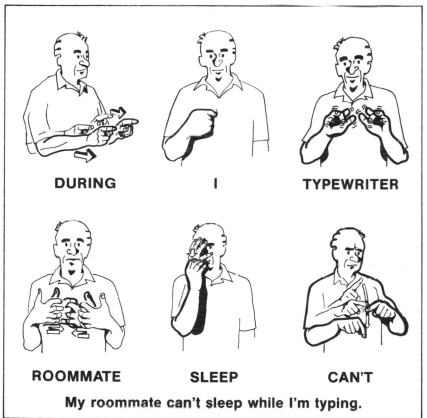

DURING **I** **TYPEWRITER**

ROOMMATE **SLEEP** **CAN'T**

My roommate can't sleep while I'm typing.

QUERY

I have a question.

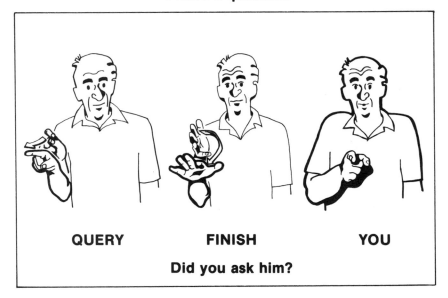

| QUERY | FINISH | YOU |

Did you ask him?

TEACH   **QUERY ME**

The teacher asked me a lot of questions.

The repetition of the QUERY sign using both hands indicates that many questions were asked.

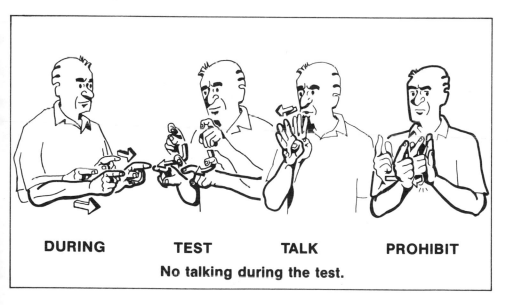

DURING   **TEST**   **TALK**   **PROHIBIT**

No talking during the test.

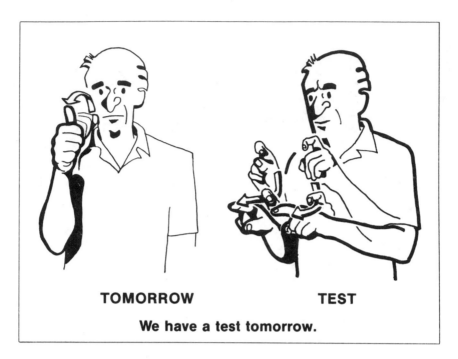

TOMORROW   **TEST**

We have a test tomorrow.

CLOSE BOOK

Close your books.

OPEN BOOK

Open your books.

WRITE   **START**

Begin writing.

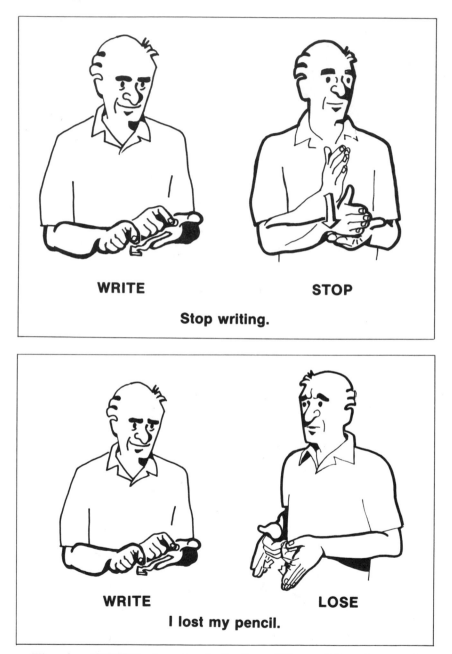

WRITE   STOP

Stop writing.

WRITE   LOSE

I lost my pencil.

The sign WRITE also stands for "pen," "pencil," and any other writing instrument.

WRITE   **AWFUL (1)**   **AWFUL (2)**   **YOU**

Your writing is terrible.

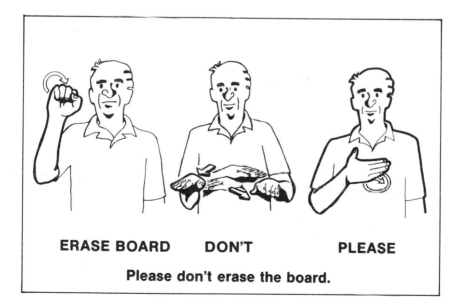

ERASE BOARD   **DON'T**   **PLEASE**

Please don't erase the board.

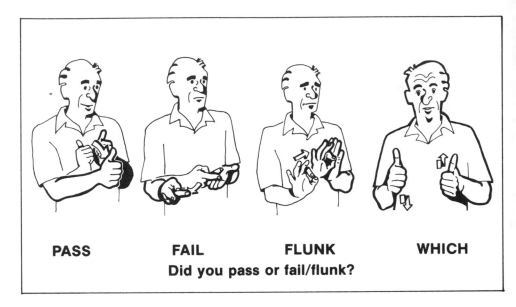

PASS   FAIL   FLUNK   WHICH

Did you pass or fail/flunk?

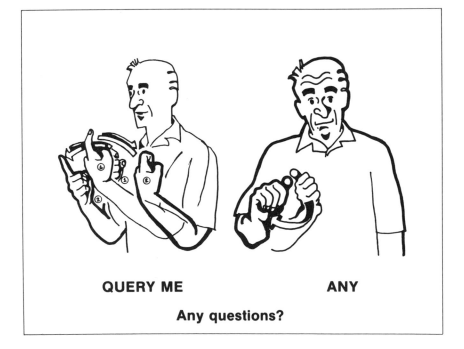

QUERY ME   ANY

Any questions?

PAPER　　**GIVE ME**　　**LATE**

You haven't turned in your paper to me yet.

In order to sign GIVE, reverse the movement of the GIVE ME sign.

WE TWO　　**DISCUSS**　　**FINISH**

She and I discussed it.

BREAK

Let's take a break.

ABSENT   EXCUSE   BRING   MUST

When you've been absent, you must bring an excuse.

Conditional statements such as "When you've eaten, you may go" or "If you're good, I'll tell you" are usually changed to questions. In the sentence shown above, the ABSENT sign is made with a questioning expression.

10

Food and Drink

EAT

FINISH

Have you eaten? Did you eat? Are you finished eating?

EAT   LATE   I

I haven't eaten yet.

HE/SHE/IT   EAT   TOO MUCH

He eats too much.

HUNGER   **YOU**

Are you hungry?

YOU AND I   **GO TO**   **RESTAURANT**

Let's you and I go to a restaurant.

ORDER   WHAT SHRUG

What are you going to order?

COCKTAIL   WANT

Do you want a cocktail?

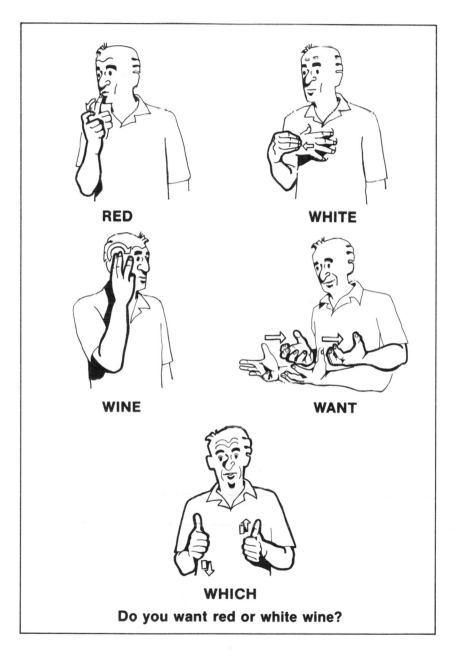

RED

WHITE

WINE

WANT

WHICH

Do you want red or white wine?

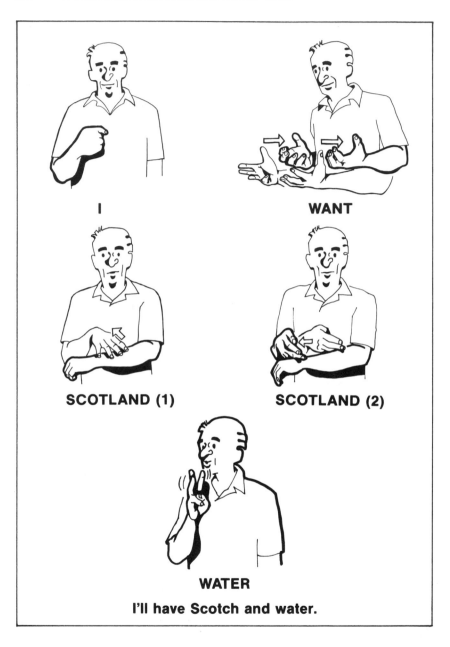

I

WANT

SCOTLAND (1)

SCOTLAND (2)

WATER

I'll have Scotch and water.

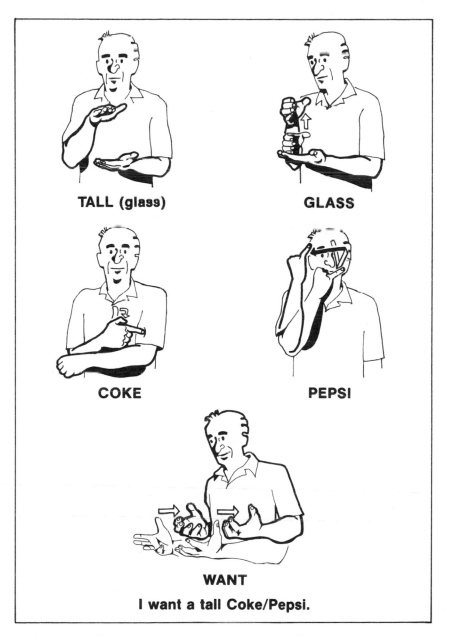

TALL (glass)

GLASS

COKE

PEPSI

WANT

I want a tall Coke/Pepsi.

Coke and Pepsi are the only soft drinks with signs; all others are fingerspelled. The same applies to Scotch and other liquors and mixed drinks. Only Scotch has a sign; the rest are fingerspelled.

SOFT DRINK (1) SOFT DRINK (2)   WANT

Do you want a soft drink?

BEER   VARIOUS   HAVE

They have a lot of different beers.

WHISKEY   **NEVER**   **HE**

He never drinks whiskey.

SANDWICH   **HAMBURGER**   **LIKE**   **I**

I like sandwiches and hamburgers.

SERVE   **AGENT**   **WHERE**

Where's the waiter/waitress?

SERVE   **LOUSY**

The service is lousy.

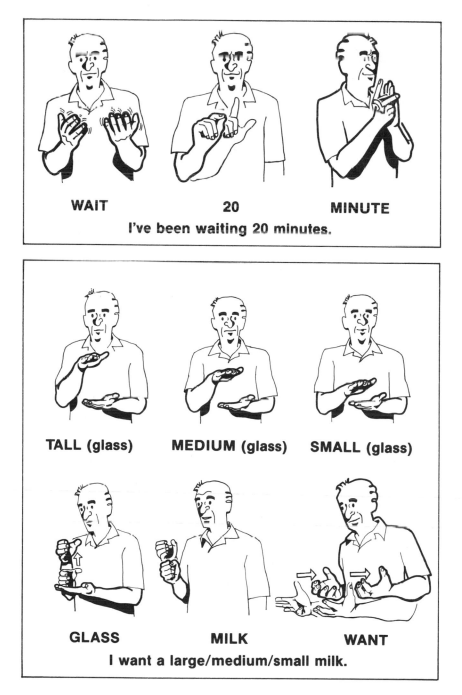

WAIT   **20**   **MINUTE**

I've been waiting 20 minutes.

TALL (glass)   **MEDIUM (glass)**   **SMALL (glass)**

GLASS   **MILK**   **WANT**

I want a large/medium/small milk.

TEA   COLD   HOT   WANT

I'll have iced/hot tea.

EAT   FINISH   COFFEE   WANT

I'll have coffee after I eat.

| MILK | CREAM | SWEET | WANT |

Do you want milk/cream and sugar?

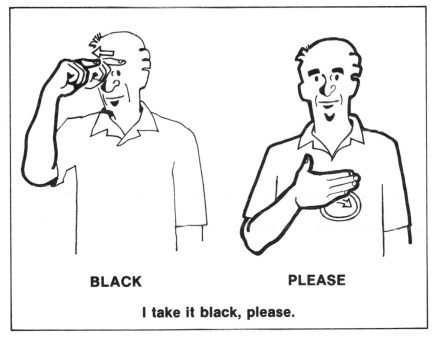

| BLACK | PLEASE |

I take it black, please.

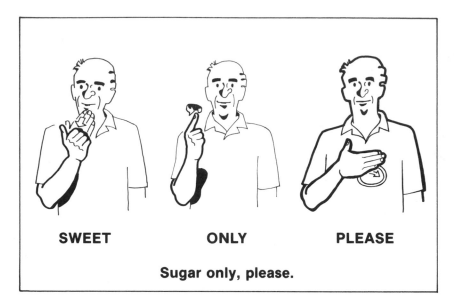

SWEET   **ONLY**   **PLEASE**

Sugar only, please.

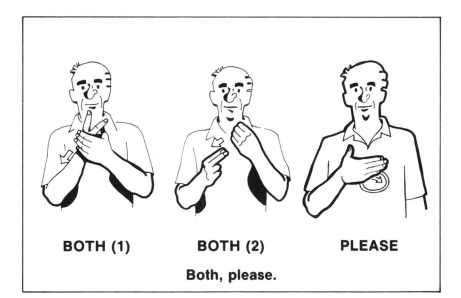

BOTH (1)   **BOTH (2)**   **PLEASE**

Both, please.

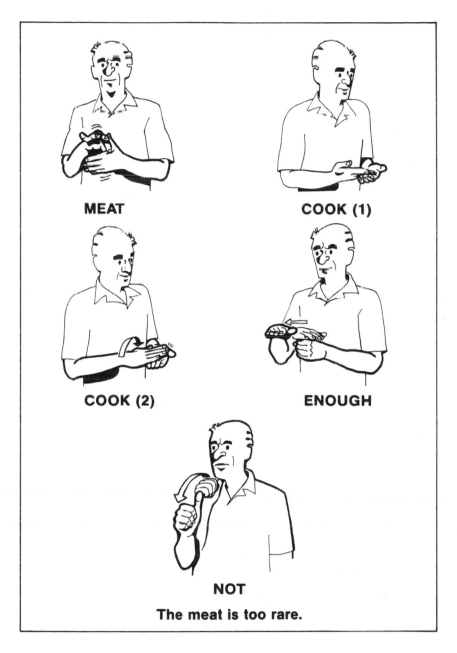

MEAT

COOK (1)

COOK (2)

ENOUGH

NOT

The meat is too rare.

V-E-G

COOK (1)

COOK (2)   TOO MUCH

The vegetables are overdone.

Fingerspell "V-E-G" at the beginning of the sentence. Most vegetables, fruits, and meats are fingerspelled. Those that have signs follow.

Additional vocabulary:

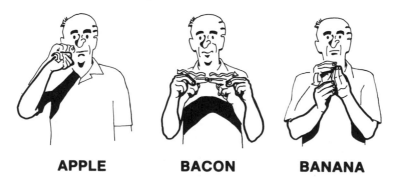

APPLE   BACON   BANANA

CABBAGE/LETTUCE   CARROT   CHICKEN (A-1)

CHICKEN (A-2)*   CHICKEN (B)   COCONUT

CORN   FISH   LEMON

*This is the sign for "BIRD," but it is often used for "chicken."

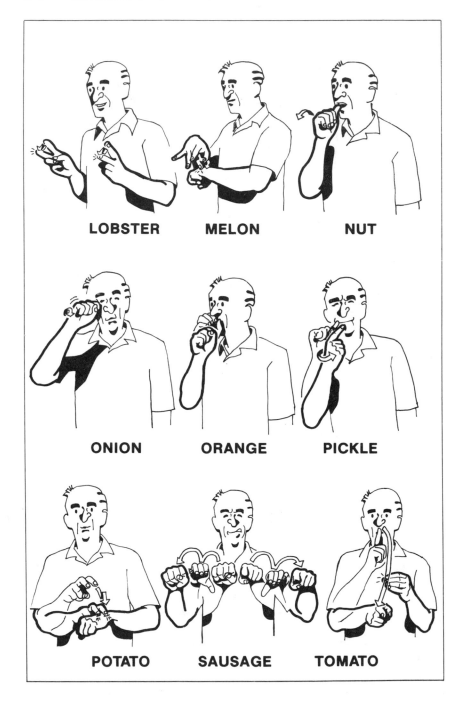

LOBSTER   MELON   NUT

ONION   ORANGE   PICKLE

POTATO   SAUSAGE   TOMATO

EAT   **DELICIOUS**

The food is delicious.

The following signs are for describing how you want your eggs.

EGG   **MIX**   **DRY**   **WET**

Scrambled.

To indicate whether you want your scrambled eggs moist or dry, sign WET or DRY after EGG MIX.

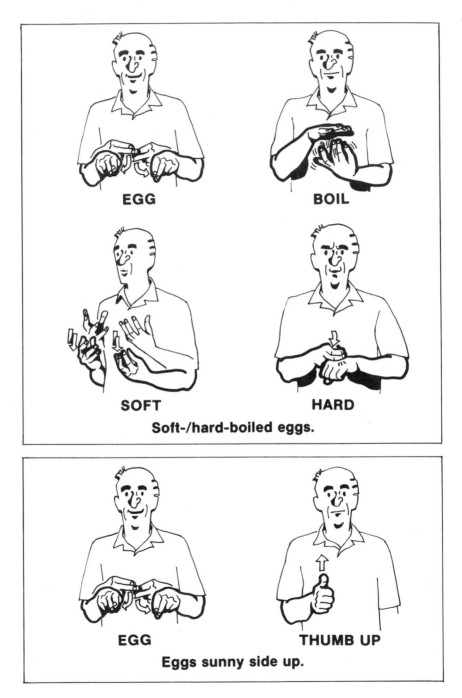

EGG

BOIL

SOFT

HARD

Soft-/hard-boiled eggs.

EGG

THUMB UP

Eggs sunny side up.

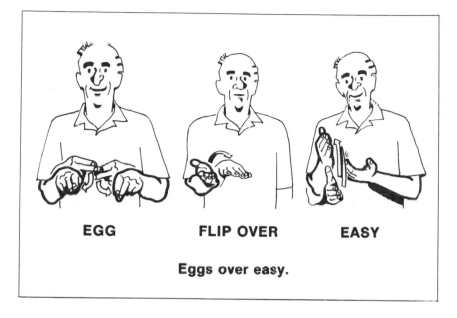

EGG   **FLIP OVER**   **EASY**

Eggs over easy.

Additional vocabulary:

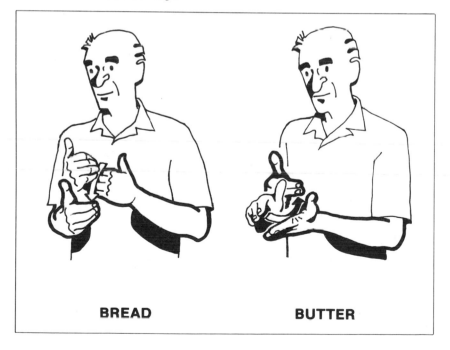

BREAD   **BUTTER**

CAKE (1)   CAKE (2)   CATSUP

DESSERT   FORK   GREASE

ICE CREAM   KNIFE   PEPPER

PIE (1)

PIE (2)

SALAD

SALT

SPOON

TOAST

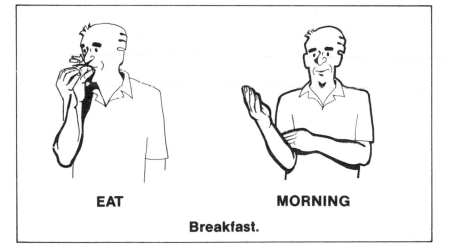

EAT

MORNING

Breakfast.

EAT   **NOON**

Lunch.

EAT   **NIGHT**

Supper/Dinner.

11
Clothing

GO TO	BUY	MUST

I have to go shopping.

The BUY sign is repeated to convey the idea "shopping."

NOW   **NIGHT**   **DRESS**   **WHAT SHRUG**

What are you wearing tonight?

DRESS   **COLOR**   **ODD**

That dress is an odd color.

DRESS   **DIRTY**   **HAVE**
Do you have any dirty clothes?

WASHING MACHINE   **MUST**
I need to do some laundry.

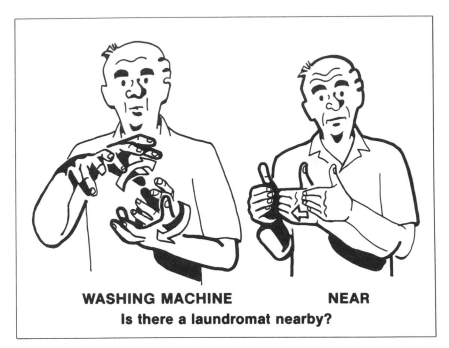

WASHING MACHINE   NEAR
Is there a laundromat nearby?

The NEAR sign is done so that the hands do not actually touch each other.

DRESS   NICE   ALWAYS   HE/SHE/IT
He always dresses nicely.

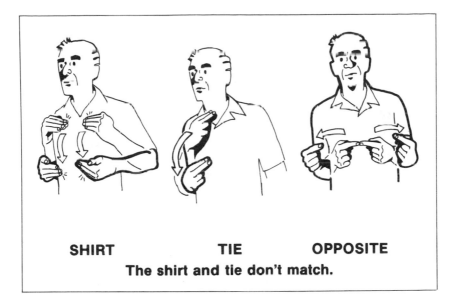

SHIRT **TIE** **OPPOSITE**
The shirt and tie don't match.

BLUE **AGREE**
Blue agrees with you.

Ordinarily the AGREE sign just moves downward, but when it is used in the expression above, it must move toward the watcher.

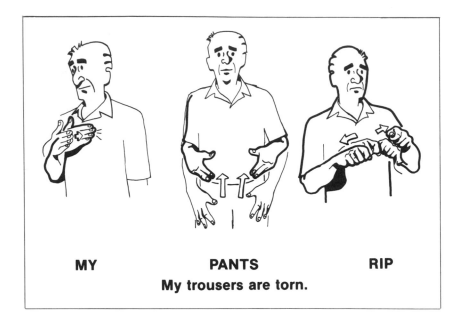

MY   **PANTS**   **RIP**

My trousers are torn.

B-U-T-T-O-N

SEW   CAN   YOU

Can you sew on a button for me?

Fingerspell BUTTON at the beginning of the sentence before the sign SEW.

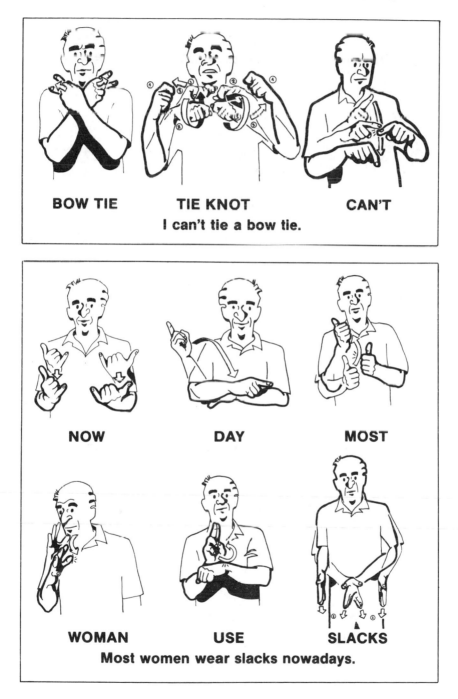

BOW TIE   **TIE KNOT**   **CAN'T**

I can't tie a bow tie.

NOW   **DAY**   **MOST**

WOMAN   **USE**   **SLACKS**

Most women wear slacks nowadays.

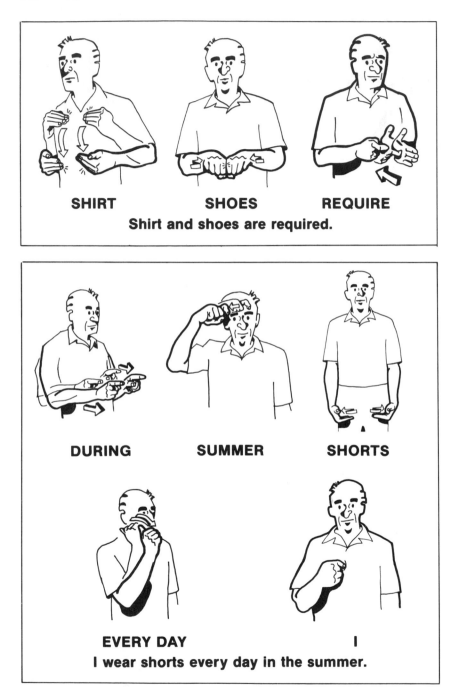

SHIRT   **SHOES**   **REQUIRE**

Shirt and shoes are required.

DURING   **SUMMER**   **SHORTS**

EVERY DAY   **I**

I wear shorts every day in the summer.

SHIRT   WASH CLOTHES   MUST
I need to wash out my shirt.

SOCKS   SAME   NOT
Your socks don't match.

MY   **HAT**   **GRAB**   **WHO**

Who took my hat?

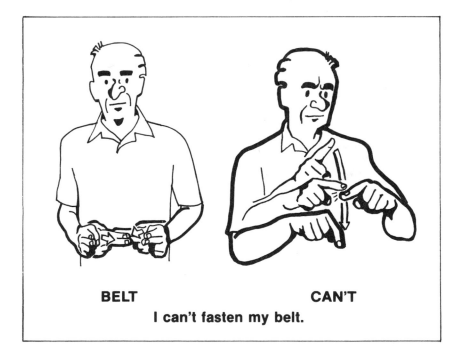

BELT   **CAN'T**

I can't fasten my belt.

COAT

PUT

CLEANERS

FINISH

SHORTER SLEEVE

When I took my coat to the cleaners, it shrunk.

12

Sports and Recreation

PLAY	BASEBALL	LIKE

Do you like to play baseball?

Additional vocabulary:

BASKETBALL	**BILLIARDS**	**CARDS**

CHECKERS	**DOMINOES**	**ELECTRONIC GAMES**

FOOTBALL	**GOLF**	**HANDBALL**

SOCCER

TABLE TENNIS

TENNIS

VOLLEYBALL

EVERY DAY   **RUN**   **I**

I run every day.

MOUNTAIN **GO TO** **FISHING** **PLEASE**

I enjoy going to the mountains to fish.

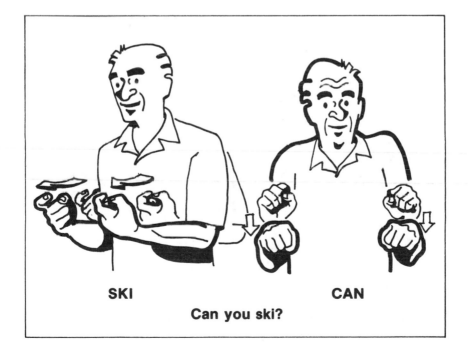

SKI **CAN**

Can you ski?

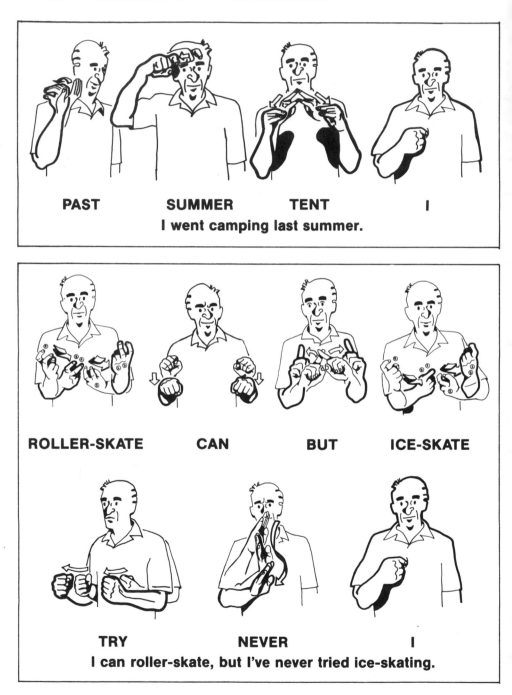

PAST   **SUMMER**   **TENT**   **I**

I went camping last summer.

ROLLER-SKATE   **CAN**   **BUT**   **ICE-SKATE**

TRY   **NEVER**   **I**

I can roller-skate, but I've never tried ice-skating.

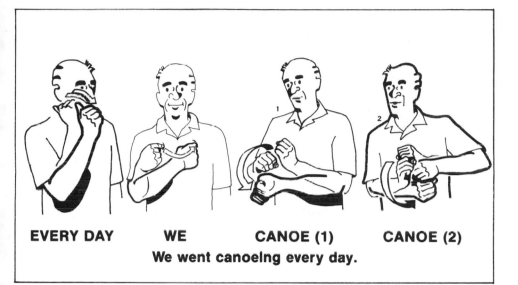

EVERY DAY   **WE**   **CANOE (1)**   **CANOE (2)**
We went canoeing every day.

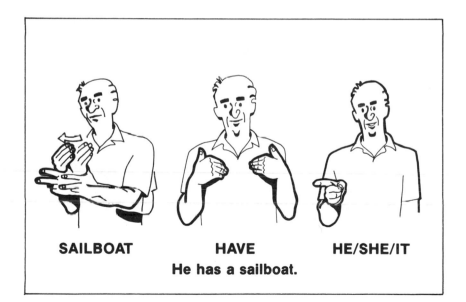

SAILBOAT   **HAVE**   **HE/SHE/IT**
He has a sailboat.

SURFBOARD   SKILL   HE/SHE/IT

She's an expert surfer.

WATER   WAVE (1)   WAVE (2)

WAVE (3)   SWIM   DON'T LIKE

I don't like to swim in the ocean.*

---

*It takes four signs to express "OCEAN"—WATER, WAVE (1), WAVE (2), and WAVE (3).

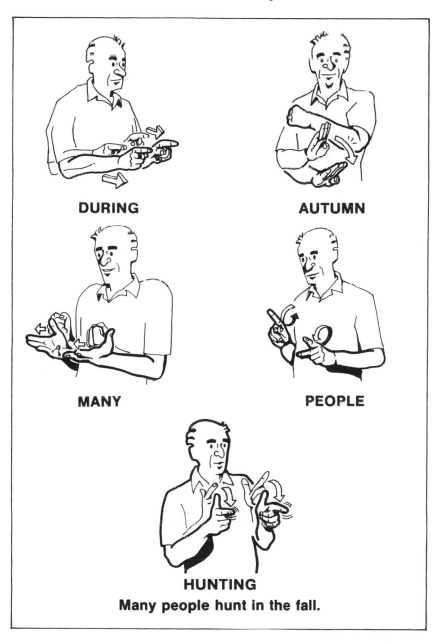

DURING

AUTUMN

MANY

PEOPLE

HUNTING

Many people hunt in the fall.

HORSE   COMPETE   BET

CRAZY   HE/SHE/IT

He's crazy about betting on the horses.

RIDE HORSE   LOVE   HE/SHE/IT

She loves to ride horses.

CHAIN (Olympics)   **COMPETE**   **HOPE**   **HE/SHE/IT**

He hopes to compete in the Olympics.

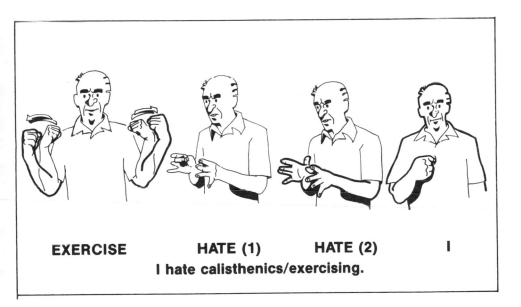

EXERCISE   **HATE (1)**   **HATE (2)**   **I**

I hate calisthenics/exercising.

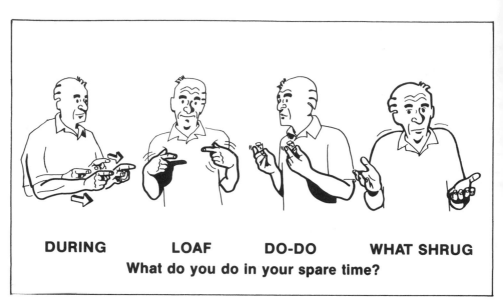

DURING   LOAF   DO-DO   WHAT SHRUG

What do you do in your spare time?

DANCE   LIKE

Do you like to dance?

DANCE **LEARN** **WANT**
Do you want to learn to dance?

STOP **REST** **NOW**
Let's stop and rest now.

WEEKLY   **BOWL**   **I**

I go bowling every week.

13

Travel

In recent years, there has been a movement among American deaf people to replace ASL signs for other nationalities with the signs used by the deaf people of those nationalities. The reasons for this were, first, to show respect for the sign language of those nationalities by using their sign. The second reason was that the ASL sign sometimes was a derogatory sign in the sign language of another country. The ASL sign for Sweden, for example, means "drunk" or "crazy" in Swedish sign language, so naturally Swedes objected to our using the sign to refer to them and their country. Japanese and Chinese deaf people did not like the ASL signs for their countries because they highlighted the slanted eyes of Asians.

The movement to replace ASL signs with the indigenous signs of other sign languages is still in its infancy. It is impossible to predict how long it will take for these "new" signs to spread among the population until they are commonly known everywhere. At the present time, they are known and used mainly in the large metropolitan centers on the East and West Coasts.

In this chapter, the signs marked with an asterisk (*) indicate the sign used by the deaf people of the nation to which the sign refers. Only those signs that are known by the international community to be truly representative of the signs used by the deaf people within the country are asterisked.

ONLY   **DAY**   **I**

GO TO   **AFRICA**
Someday I'm going to Africa.

Additional vocabulary:

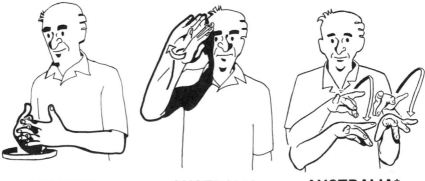

AMERICA   **AUSTRALIA**   **AUSTRALIA***

CANADA

CHINA

CHINA*

DENMARK

DENMARK*

EGYPT

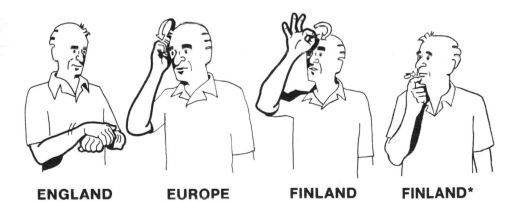

ENGLAND   **EUROPE**   **FINLAND**   **FINLAND***

FRANCE

GERMANY

GERMANY*

GREECE

HAWAII

HOLLAND

HOLLAND*   **INDIA**   **IRELAND**

ISRAEL

ITALY

ITALY*

JAPAN

JAPAN*

MEXICO

NORWAY

NORWAY*

POLAND

RUSSIA

SPAIN

SCOTLAND (1)

SCOTLAND (2)

SCOTLAND*

SWEDEN

SWEDEN*

TOUCH **FINISH** **JAPAN** **YOU**
Have you ever been to Japan?

NOW **NIGHT** **AIRPLANE** **NEW YORK**
I'm flying to New York tonight.

Almost every city has a sign, or a fingerspelled abbreviation. Often, however, the sign is either not common outside the state or it is the same sign for another city in another state. For example,

Berkeley and Boston share the same sign. Therefore, one must inquire of local deaf people how the cities in their state are signed. A few cities do have signs that are used all over the country. New York is one such city, and others are shown below:

ATLANTA   **CHICAGO**   **MILWAUKEE**

NEW ORLEANS   **PHILADELPHIA**   **PITTSBURGH**

SAN FRANCISCO   **WASHINGTON**

San Francisco is abbreviated to "SF," and so are many other cities. Take care with Los Angeles, since its abbreviation can also mean Louisiana.

PACK BAGS   **FINISH**
Are your bags packed?

I   BRING   AIRPLANE

I'll take you to the airport.

AIRPLANE   NAME   WHICH

Which airline are you taking?

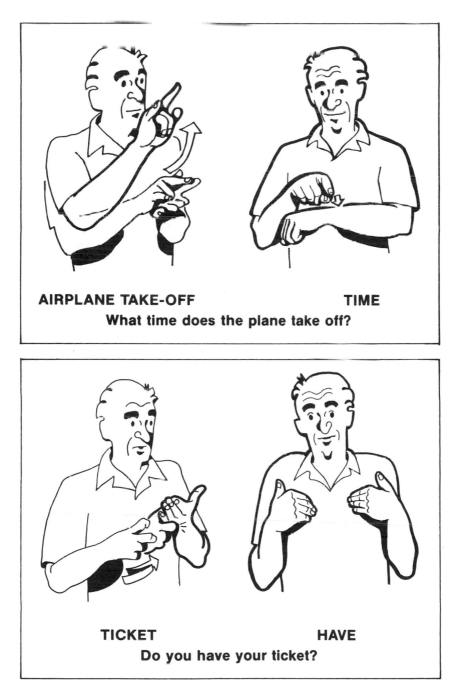

AIRPLANE TAKE-OFF　　　　　　　　　**TIME**
What time does the plane take off?

TICKET　　　　　　　　　**HAVE**
Do you have your ticket?

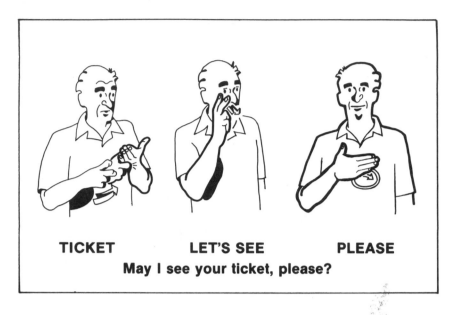

TICKET   LET'S SEE   PLEASE
May I see your ticket, please?

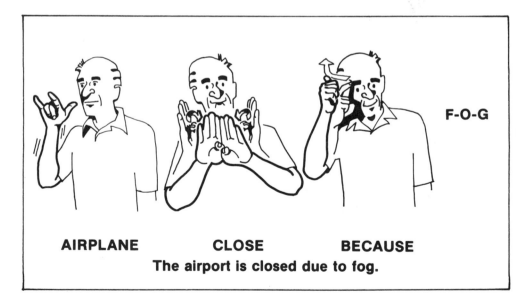

F-O-G

AIRPLANE   CLOSE   BECAUSE
The airport is closed due to fog.

There is no sign for "fog," so fingerspell it at the end of the sentence, after the sign BECAUSE.

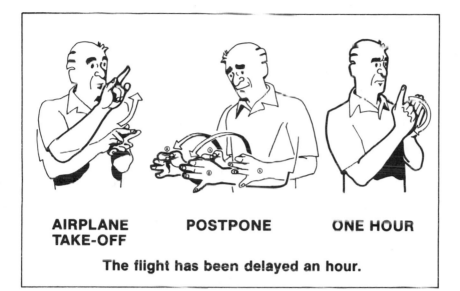

AIRPLANE TAKE-OFF   **POSTPONE**   **ONE HOUR**

The flight has been delayed an hour.

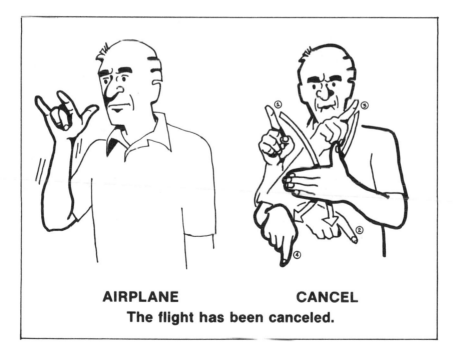

AIRPLANE   **CANCEL**

The flight has been canceled.

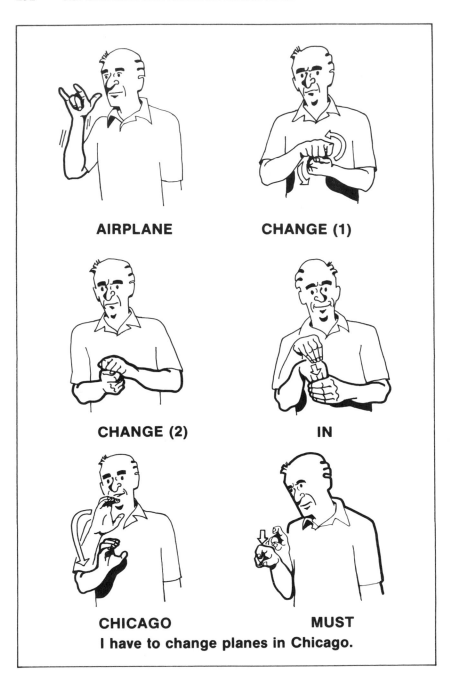

AIRPLANE

CHANGE (1)

CHANGE (2)

IN

CHICAGO

MUST

I have to change planes in Chicago.

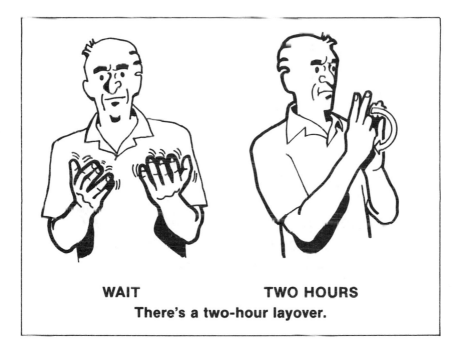

WAIT   **TWO HOURS**
There's a two-hour layover.

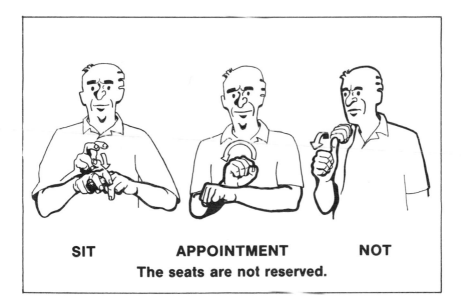

SIT   **APPOINTMENT**   **NOT**
The seats are not reserved.

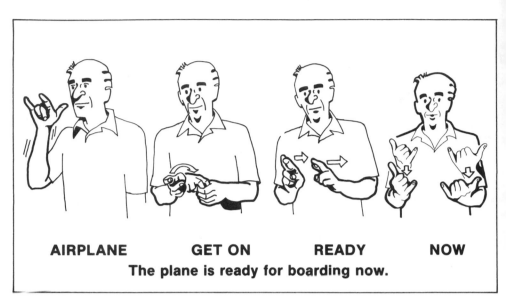

AIRPLANE   GET ON   READY   NOW
The plane is ready for boarding now.

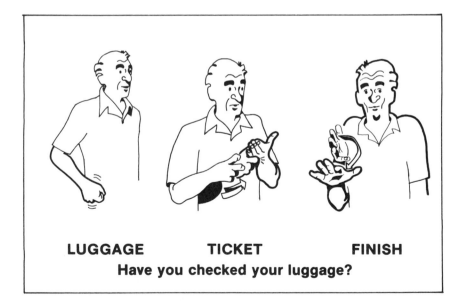

LUGGAGE   TICKET   FINISH
Have you checked your luggage?

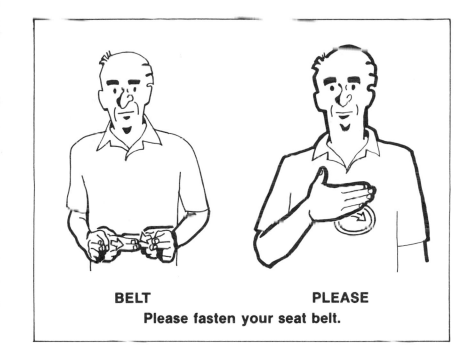

BELT   PLEASE

Please fasten your seat belt.

MAGAZINE   NEWSPAPER (1) NEWSPAPER (2)   WANT

Would you like a magazine or newspaper?

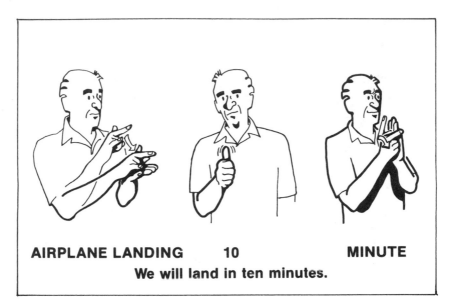

AIRPLANE LANDING   10   MINUTE

We will land in ten minutes.

ONLY   MEET   YOU

Is somebody meeting you?

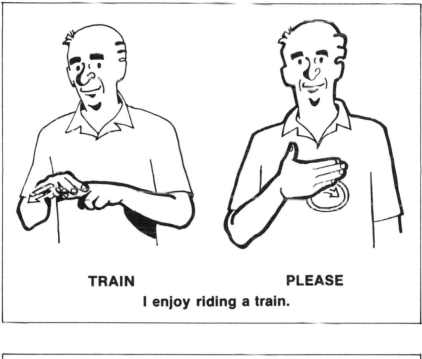

TRAIN **PLEASE**
I enjoy riding a train.

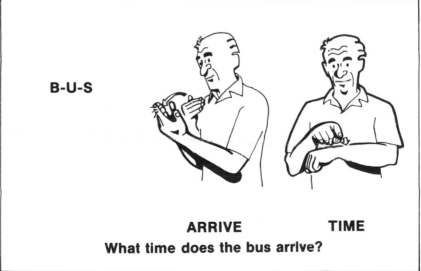

B-U-S

ARRIVE **TIME**
What time does the bus arrive?

There is no sign for "bus," so fingerspell it at the beginning of the sentence before the sign ARRIVE.

TRAIN   DEPART   TIME
What time does the train leave?

TICKET   BUY   FINISH
Have you bought your ticket?

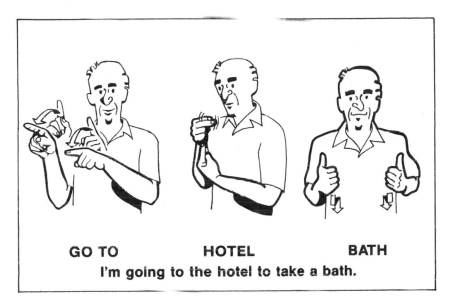

GO TO   **HOTEL**   **BATH**

I'm going to the hotel to take a bath.

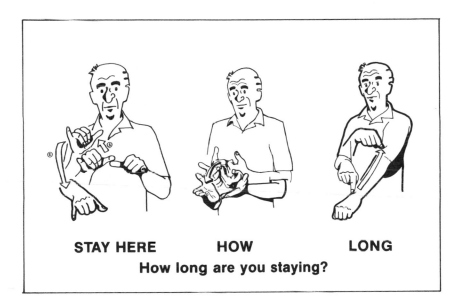

STAY HERE   **HOW**   **LONG**

How long are you staying?

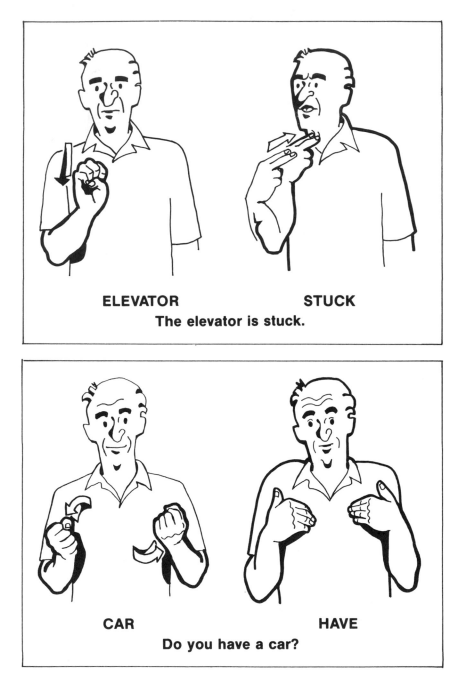

ELEVATOR   STUCK
The elevator is stuck.

CAR   HAVE
Do you have a car?

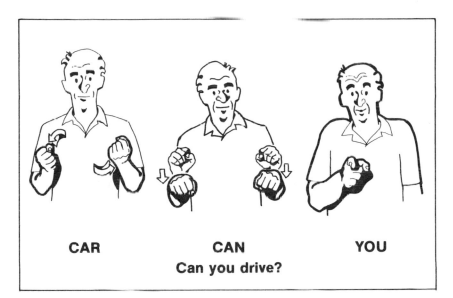

CAR   **CAN**   **YOU**

Can you drive?

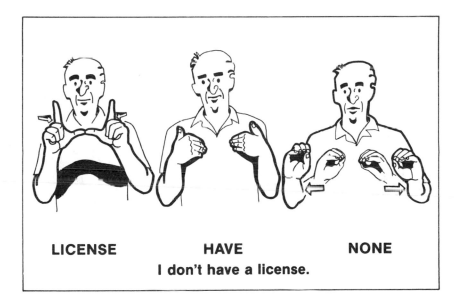

LICENSE   **HAVE**   **NONE**

I don't have a license.

SHIFT   KNOW   HOW

Do you know how to use a manual shift?

VEHICLE (park)   HERE   ALL NIGHT   PROHIBIT

It's illegal to park here overnight.

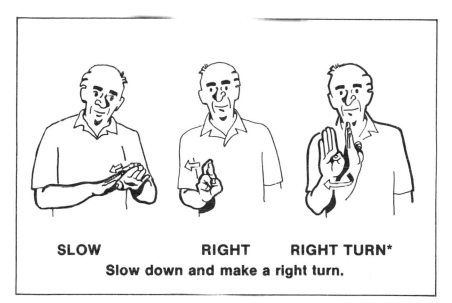

SLOW **RIGHT** **RIGHT TURN***
Slow down and make a right turn.

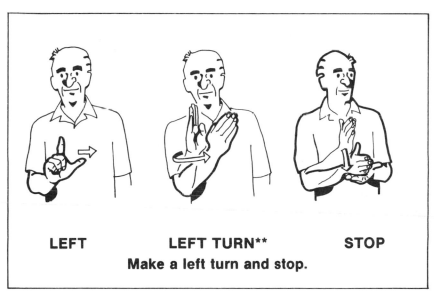

LEFT **LEFT TURN**** **STOP**
Make a left turn and stop.

*"RIGHT" means "as opposed to left," but "RIGHT TURN" is one sign.

**"LEFT" means "as opposed to right," but "LEFT TURN" is one sign.

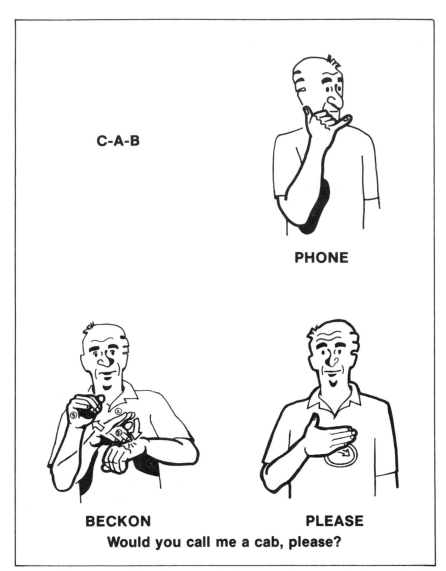

C-A-B

PHONE

BECKON   PLEASE

Would you call me a cab, please?

There is no sign for "cab," so fingerspell it at the beginning of the sentence, before the sign PHONE.

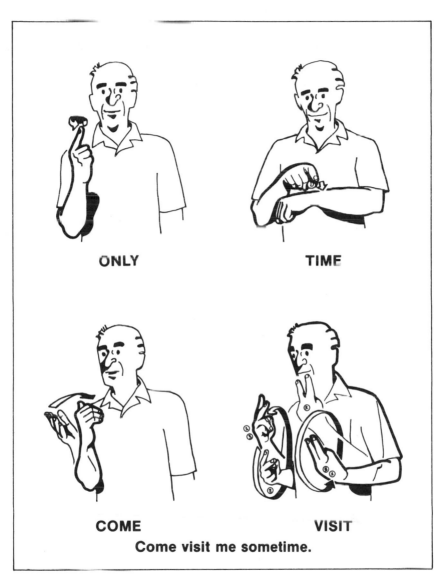

ONLY

TIME

COME

VISIT

Come visit me sometime.

Almost all states are fingerspelled using the standard written abbreviations such as Penn. or Pa., N.D., and Wyo. States such as Ohio that have short names are spelled out. The few states that have signs that are used throughout the country are shown below:

ARIZONA   **CALIFORNIA**   **HAWAII**

NEW YORK   **TEXAS**   **WASHINGTON**

14

Animals, Colors

ANIMALS

ASL does not have a sign for every animal. Presented here are nearly all the animal signs that do exist. All other animal names are either fingerspelled or have signs that are known only in a particular area.

ANIMAL   **ALLIGATOR (1)**   **ALLIGATOR (2)**

BEAR (1)

BEAR (2)

BEE (1)

BEE (2)

BIRD (1)

BIRD (2)

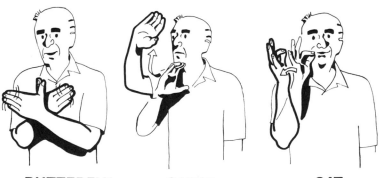

BUTTERFLY   **CAMEL**   **CAT**

CHICKEN*   **COW**   **DEER**

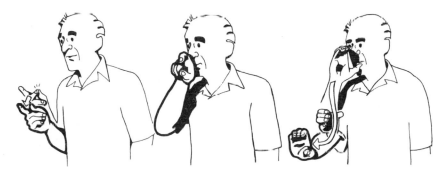

DOG   **EAGLE**   **ELEPHANT (A)**

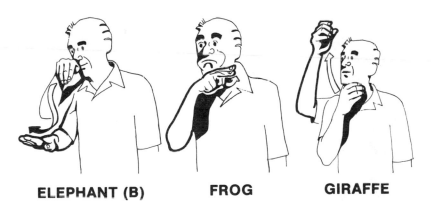

ELEPHANT (B)   **FROG**   **GIRAFFE**

*While this sign means "chicken," the sign "BIRD" is also often used to mean "chicken."

GOAT   **HAWK**   **HORSE**

INSECT   **LION**   **MONKEY**

MOUSE   **MULE**   **RABBIT (A)**

RABBIT (B)

RAT

SHEEP

SNAKE

TIGER

WORM

TURKEY (A-1)

TURKEY (A-2)

TURKEY (B)

COLORS

ASL does not have a sign for every color, so "beige" and "fuchsia" have to be fingerspelled. Colors such as "blue-green," however, may be signed by combining the two signs BLUE and GREEN.

BLACK   **BLUE**   **BROWN**

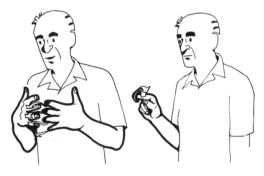

GRAY (1)   **GRAY (2)**   **GREEN**

ORANGE PINK PURPLE

RED WHITE YELLOW

Varying shades of colors can be signed by using the signs DARK and CLEAR. In this sense, CLEAR means "light."

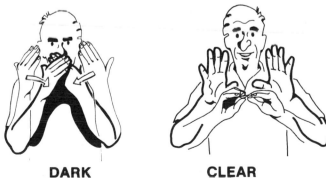

DARK CLEAR

15
Civics

DEMOCRAT   REPUBLICAN   INDEPENDENT   I
I'm a Democrat/Republican/Independent.

VOTE   **FINISH**   **I**   **YOU**

I voted, did you?

NEW   **PRESIDENT**   **WHO**

Who's the new president?

VOTE   **WIN**   **WHO**
Who won the election?

LAW   **PASS**   **RESPONSIBLE**

WHO   **LEGISLATURE**   **CONGRESS**
The legislature/congress is responsible for passing laws.

This is an example of the rhetorical question, where the signer asks, then answers, the question. It is used a great deal in ASL. There is a slight pause at the end of the question—after the sign WHO in this example—and then the answer is signed.

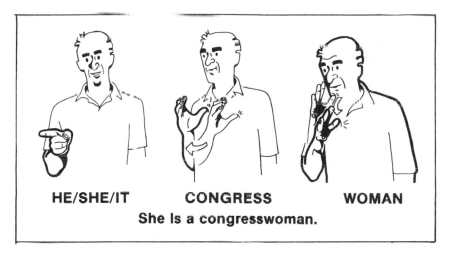

HE/SHE/IT   CONGRESS   WOMAN

She Is a congresswoman.

The AGENT sign shown below is usually done following the SENATE, GOVERNMENT, JUDGE, and LAW signs to indicate senator, governor, judge, and lawyer, respectively. (See the discussion of the AGENT sign in the Dictionary/Index, page 327.)

HE/SHE/IT   SENATE   GOVERNMENT

JUDGE   LAW   AGENT

He is a senator/governor/judge/lawyer.

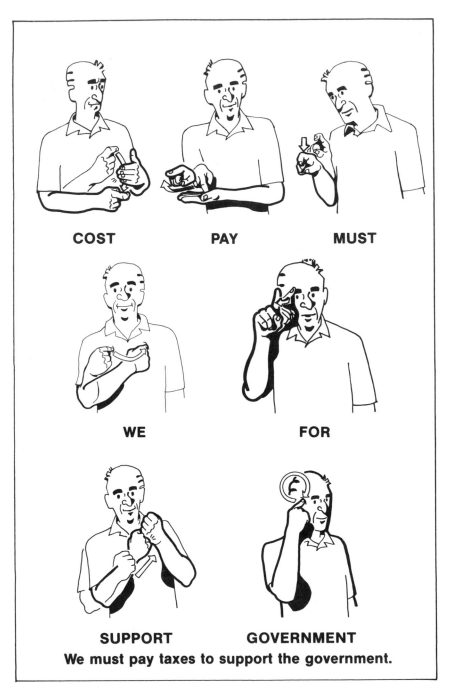

COST   PAY   MUST

WE   FOR

SUPPORT   GOVERNMENT

We must pay taxes to support the government.

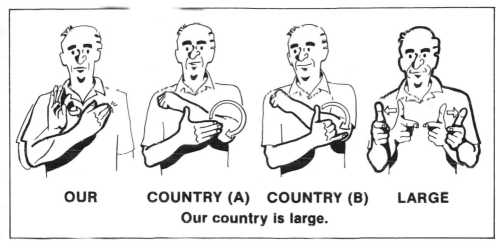

OUR COUNTRY (A) COUNTRY (B) LARGE
Our country is large.

Either sign for "country" is acceptable.

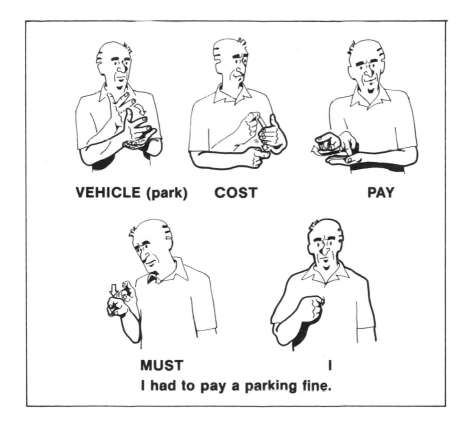

VEHICLE (park) COST PAY

MUST I
I had to pay a parking fine.

GOVERNMENT   CITY   NAME   WHAT SHRUG
Which city is the capitol?

LAW   BREAK   JAIL   MAYBE
If you break the law, you might go to jail.

The idea of "if" is often expressed in ASL by stating the sentence as a question. This requires a questioning expression. In the above sentence the expression would be done on the BREAK sign, and then there is a slight pause before you sign the consequence. In the following sentence, the questioning expression happens with the DISOBEY sign, which is followed by a pause before the rest of the statement is signed.

LAW   **DISOBEY**   **PUNISH**   **WILL**

If you disobey the law, you will be punished.

LAW   **OBEY**   **MUST**   **YOU**

You must obey the law.

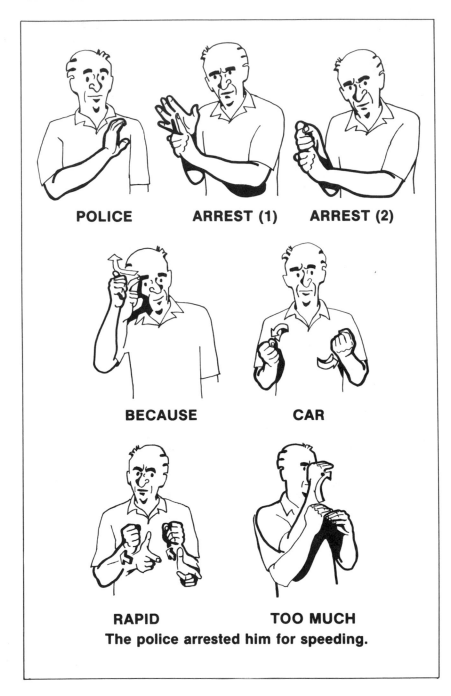

POLICE   ARREST (1)   ARREST (2)

BECAUSE   CAR

RAPID   TOO MUCH

The police arrested him for speeding.

HE/SHE/IT   **PLAN**   **AGAINST**
She plans to sue them.

THEY   **PROTEST**   **AGAINST**
They are on strike against the company.

There is no sign for "company," so fingerspell C-O at the end of the sentence after the sign AGAINST.

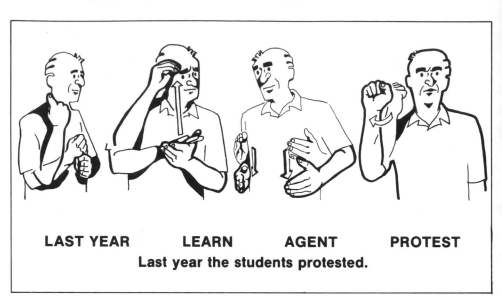

LAST YEAR   **LEARN**   **AGENT**   **PROTEST**

Last year the students protested.

PICKET   **ALL MORNING**   **I**

I was on the picket line all morning.

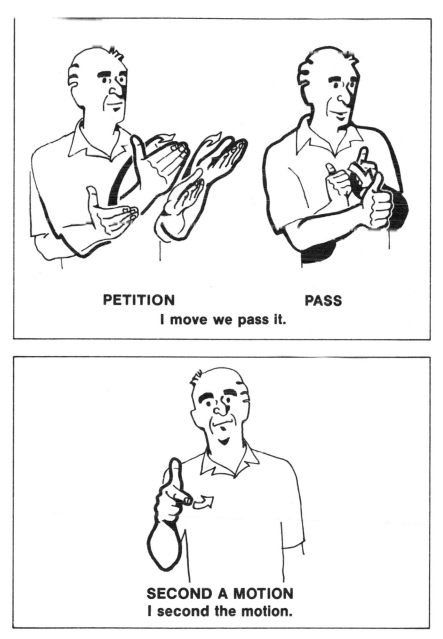

PETITION   **PASS**
I move we pass it.

SECOND A MOTION
I second the motion.

This sign is also used idiomatically to show that you agree with someone.

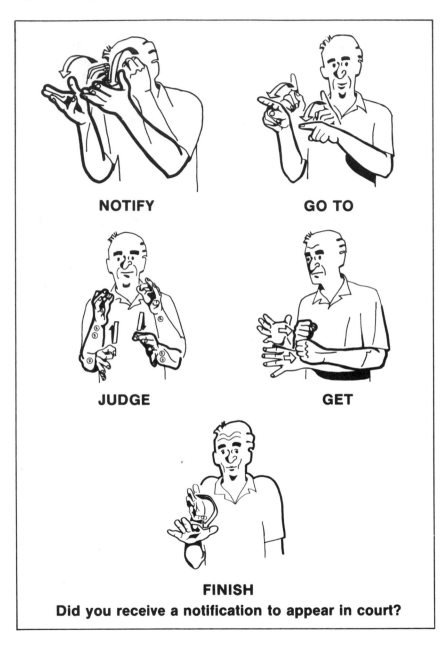

NOTIFY

GO TO

JUDGE

GET

FINISH
Did you receive a notification to appear in court?

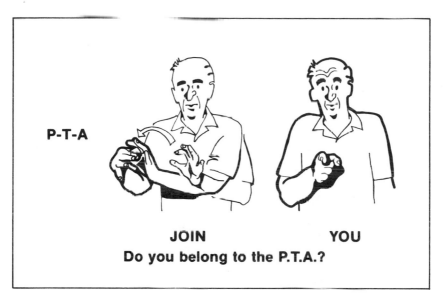

P-T-A

JOIN **YOU**
Do you belong to the P.T.A.?

There is no sign for "P.T.A.," so fingerspell it at the beginning of the sentence before the sign JOIN.

S-S

PENSION **HE/SHE/IT**
He's on Social Security.

Fingerspell "S-S" to indicate "social security" at the beginning of the sentence before the sign PENSION.

S-S-I

PENSION   **HE/SHE/IT**

She gets Supplementary Salary Income.

Fingerspell "S-S-I" to indicate "Supplementary Salary Income" at the beginning of the sentence before the sign PENSION.

JUDGE   **GO TO**   **GOOD**

LAW   **AGENT**

MUST   **YOU**

If you go to court, you should have a good lawyer.

Do not forget the questioning facial expression, since this is an "if" statement. It should occur with the sign GO TO.

16

Religion

Signs for various denominations differ considerably around the country, so it is suggested that you make local inquiries about how specific denominations are signed in your area. Those that follow are fairly standard.

CHRIST   AGENT   YOU

Are you a Christian?

JEWISH   **OLD**   **RELIGION**

Judaism is an old religion.

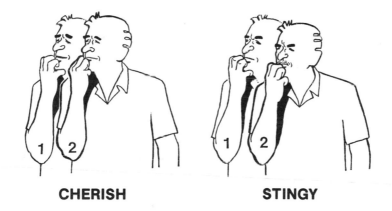

CHERISH   **STINGY**

Although the signs CHERISH and STINGY are very similar, the facial expression is quite different in each case, naturally. The sign JEWISH looks as if you are stroking a beard. It would, obviously, be offensive if you signed STINGY and meant to sign JEWISH, so be careful.

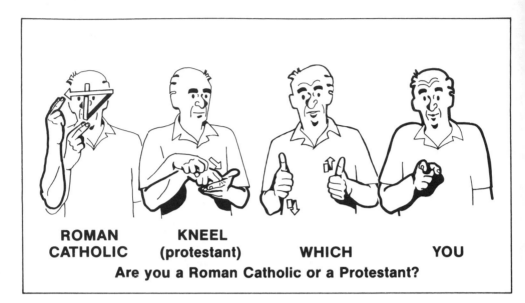

ROMAN CATHOLIC   **KNEEL (protestant)**   **WHICH**   **YOU**

Are you a Roman Catholic or a Protestant?

DISBELIEVE   **HE/SHE/IT**

He's an atheist.

BAPTIZE (Baptist)

EPISCOPAL

LUTHERAN

MORMON

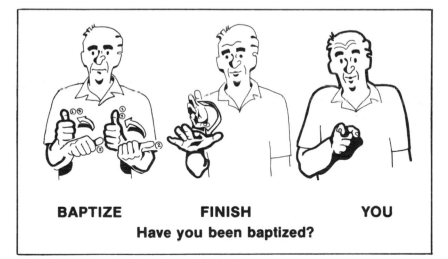

BAPTIZE　　　**FINISH**　　　**YOU**

Have you been baptized?

If a particular denomination baptizes by sprinkling rather than by immersion, then one of the following signs is used:

BAPTIZE (A)   **BAPTIZE (B)**

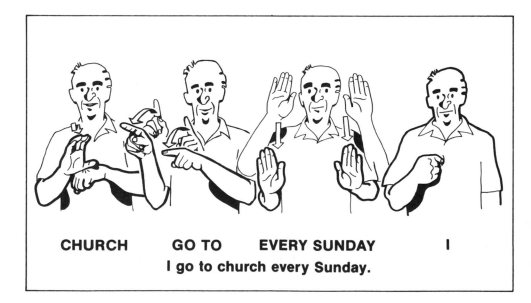

CHURCH   GO TO   EVERY SUNDAY   I
I go to church every Sunday.

JEWISH   **GO TO**   **TEMPLE**   **SATURDAY**

Jewish people go to temple on the Sabbath.

CHURCH   **JOIN**   **WHICH**

Which church do you belong to?

LONG AGO   PREACH   HE/SHE/IT
He used to be a preacher.

MISSIONARY   HE/SHE/IT
She's a missionary.

ME

INTERPRET (1)

INTERPRET (2)

PREACH

WANT

YOU

Do you want me to interpret the sermon?

Additional vocabulary:

ANGEL   **BELIEVE**   **BLESS**

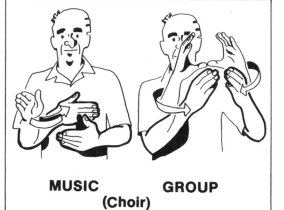

MUSIC   **GROUP**   **COMMUNION**
(Choir)

CONFESSION   **CRUCIFY (1)**   **CRUCIFY (2)**

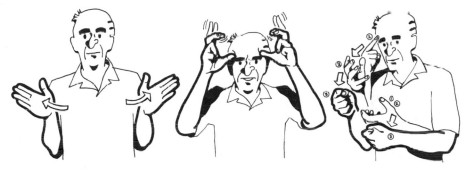

CRUCIFY (3)   **DEVIL**   **FAITH**

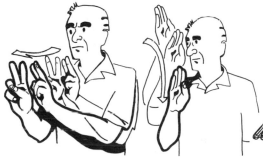

FUNERAL   **GOD**   **GRAVE**

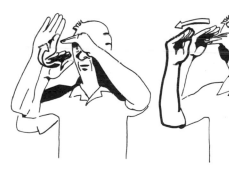

HEAVEN (1)   **HEAVEN (2)**   **HELL**

JESUS (1)

JESUS (2)

LORD

MASS

CRACKER (Passover)

PITY

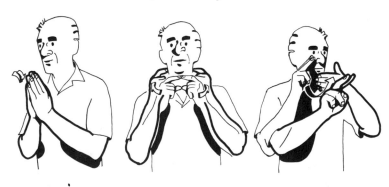

PRAY   **PRIEST**   **PROPHECY**

RABBI

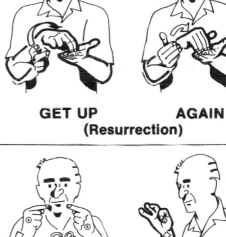

GET UP
(Resurrection)

AGAIN

SAVE

SIN

SOUL (A)

SOUL (B-1)

SOUL (B-2)

WORSHIP

17

Numbers, Time, Dates, and Money

NUMBERS

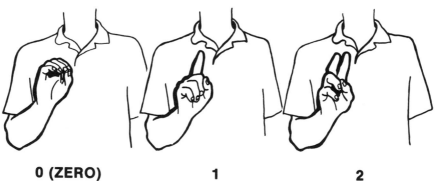

0 (ZERO)   1   2

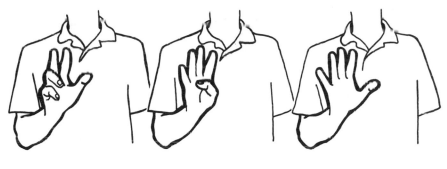

3   4   5

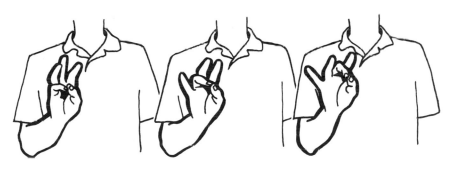

6   7   8

9

The signs for the number 6 and the letter W are exactly the same, and the sign for the number 9 is the same as that for the letter F. Context tells you whether the number or the letter is intended.

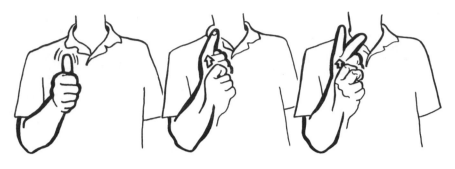

10   **11**   **12**

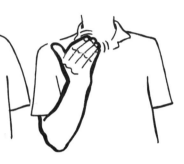

13   **14**   **15**

16   **17**   **18**

19

The numbers 16 through 19 are actually a very fast blend of 10 and 6, 10 and 7, 10 and 8, 10 and 9.

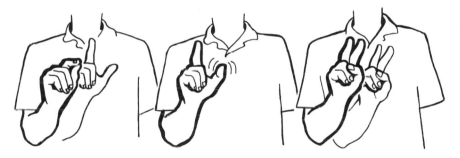

20   **21**   **22**

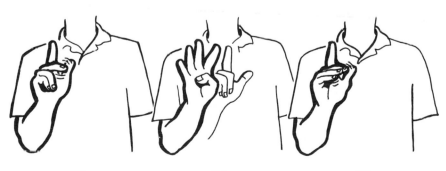

23   **24**   **25**

26

27

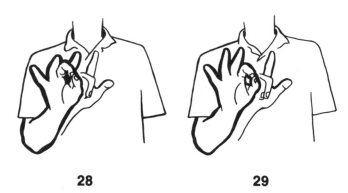

28

29

That the "2" in the twenties is made with the thumb and index finger rather than the index and second fingers—as it appears in the number 22—is probably due to the fact that ASL has its roots in the old French sign language. In Europe, even hearing people count *one* with the thumb, and *two* with the thumb and index finger.

The remaining numbers from 30 through 99 are done with the numbers 0 through 9. Examples follow:

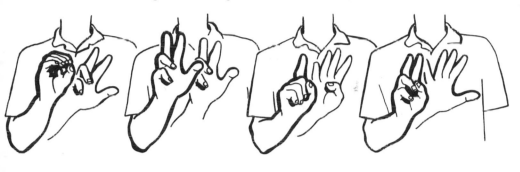

| 30 | 33 | 41 | 52 |

| 64 | 75 | 86 |

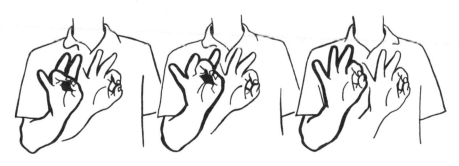

| 97 | 98 | 99 |

The number 100 is made by signing the number 1 and the letter C:

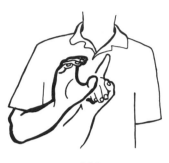

100

The numbers between 100 and 999 are made in one of two ways. One may make the number "7-7-7" or one may sign "7-C-7-7":

777 (A)   **777 (B)**

The numbers 1,000 and 1,000,000 are signed like so:

1,000   **1,000,000**

Fractions are made the same way they are written, one number above another:

½ (A)

The one-half sign as shown above is usually made more quickly as shown below:

½ (B)   ¾

Percentages are made as follows:

10   per cent (%)
10 per cent.

Numbers with decimals can also be expressed:

1-.7-5
1.75

The sign for the decimal may also mean the punctuation mark "period."

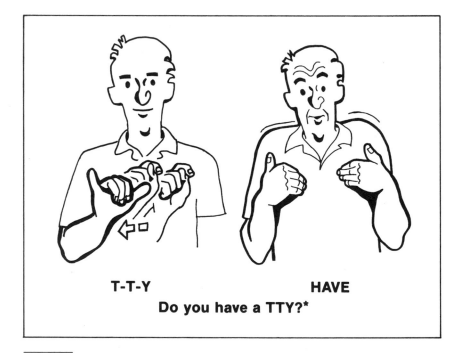

T-T-Y   **HAVE**
Do you have a TTY?*

---

*The TTY or TDD is a device that permits one to type messages back and forth over the telephone.

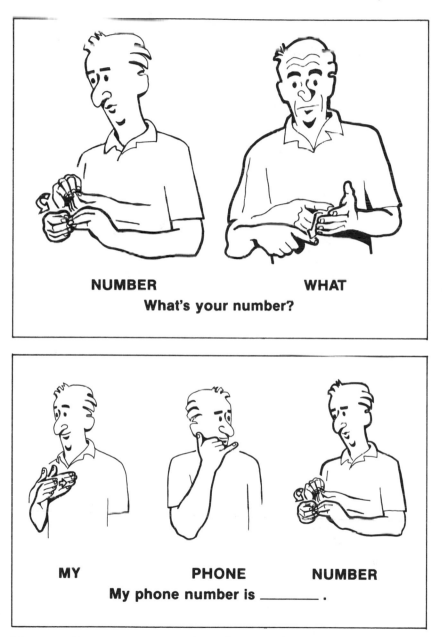

NUMBER   **WHAT**

What's your number?

MY   **PHONE**   **NUMBER**

My phone number is _____ .

Fingerspell your phone number after the sign NUMBER.

TIME

Telling time in ASL is usually done exactly in the same way as it is done in English.

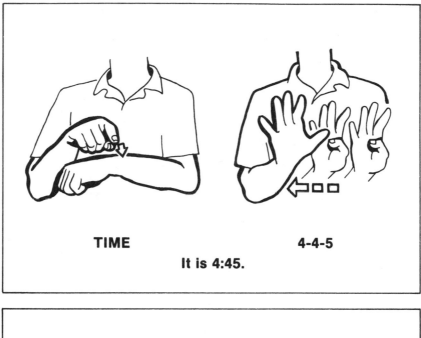

TIME   **4-4-5**

It is 4:45.

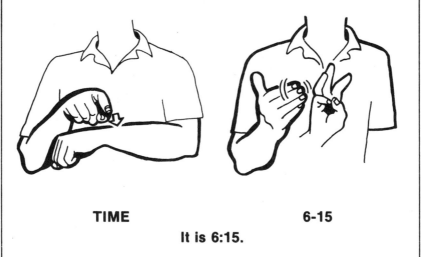

TIME   **6-15**

It is 6:15.

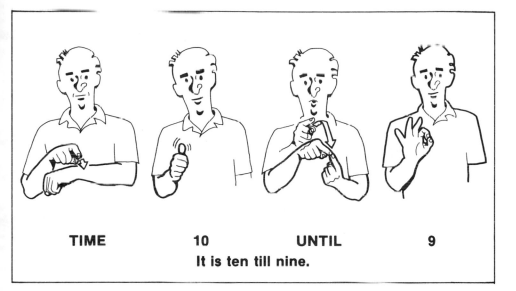

TIME   **10**   **UNTIL**   **9**

It is ten till nine.

DATES

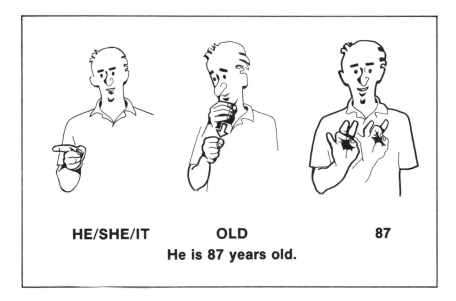

HE/SHE/IT   **OLD**   **87**

He is 87 years old.

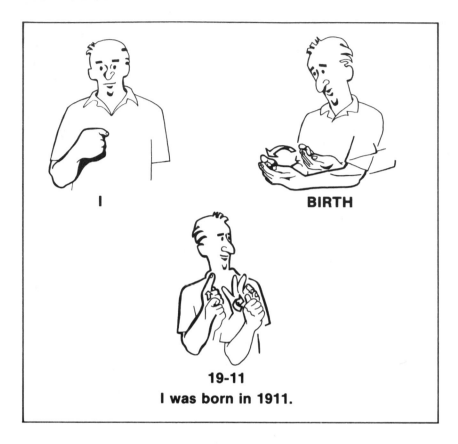

I

BIRTH

19-11
I was born in 1911.

Most of the months are abbreviated in fingerspelling. Only the short ones—March, April, May, June, and July—are spelled out completely.

MY

BIRTH

DAY

3

A-P-R-I-L

19-48

My birthday is April 3, 1948.

MONDAY   **TUESDAY**   **WEDNESDAY**

THURSDAY   **FRIDAY**   **SATURDAY**

WONDERFUL   **WEEK**   **LAST WEEK**
(Sunday)

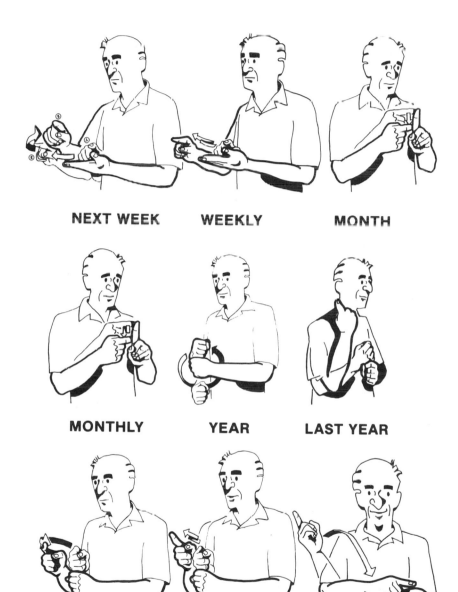

NEXT WEEK   WEEKLY   MONTH

MONTHLY   YEAR   LAST YEAR

NEXT YEAR   ANNUAL   DAY

ALL DAY   **NIGHT**   **ALL NIGHT**

MORNING   **NOON**   **AFTERNOON**

EVERY DAY   **GROW (spring)**   **SUMMER**

AUTUMN

COLD (winter)

| **SEE** | **NEAR FUTURE** | **MONDAY** |

I'll see you next Monday.

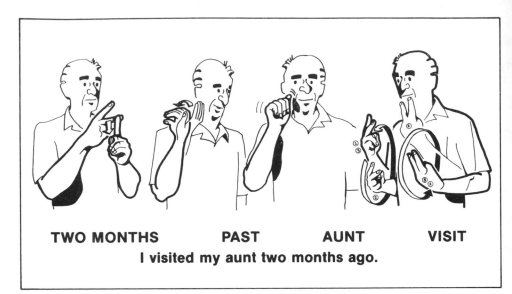

TWO MONTHS   PAST   AUNT   VISIT

I visited my aunt two months ago.

TWO YEARS AGO   BUY   NEW   HOUSE

I bought a new house two years ago.

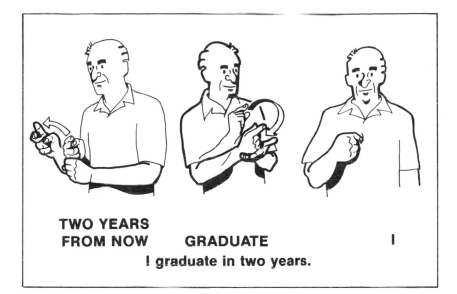

TWO YEARS FROM NOW   **GRADUATE**   **I**

I graduate in two years.

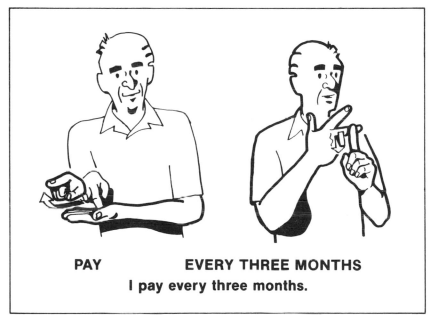

PAY   **EVERY THREE MONTHS**

I pay every three months.

EVERY
TUESDAY   **GO TO**   **MOVIE**   **HE/SHE/IT**

He goes to the movies every Tuesday.

By moving the sign for a day of the week downward, as done with TUESDAY here, you convey the idea of every week on that day.

EVERY SATURDAY   SEE

I see her every Saturday.

J-U-L-Y

4TH   **VACATION**

The fourth of July is a holiday.

Fingerspell JULY at the beginning of the sentence before the sign 4TH.

HAVE   **NICE**   **THANKSGIVING** **THANKSGIVING**
                                    (1)   **(2)**

Have a nice Thanksgiving.

HAPPY   CHRISTMAS

Merry Christmas.

HAPPY   HANUKKAH

Happy Hanukkah.

HAPPY   **NEW**   **YEAR**
Happy New Year.

HAPPY   **BIRTH**   **DAY**
Happy birthday.

MONEY

These signs also serve as ordinal numbers—i.e., first, second, third, etc.

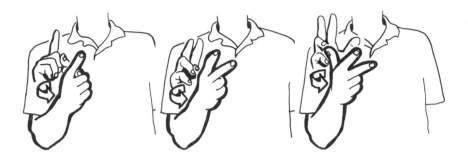

| $1.00 | $2.00 | $3.00 |

| $4.00 | $5.00 | $6.00 |

| $7.00 | $8.00 | $9.00 |

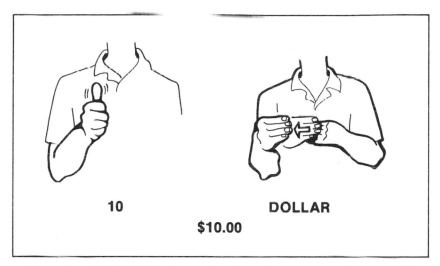

10

DOLLAR

$10.00

The sign DOLLAR is used when the amount is over nine dollars or when speaking specifically of a bill, as in "a dollar bill."

1¢

2¢

3¢

4¢

5¢

6¢

7¢   8¢

9¢   10¢

These signs are used only when speaking of these amounts by themselves, not when they are preceded by a dollar amount. For example, $3.09 would be signed as follows:

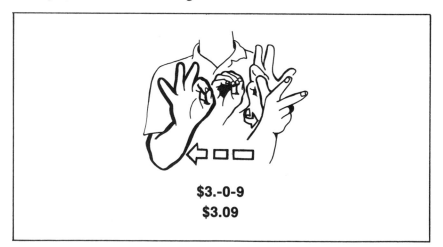

$3.-0-9
$3.09

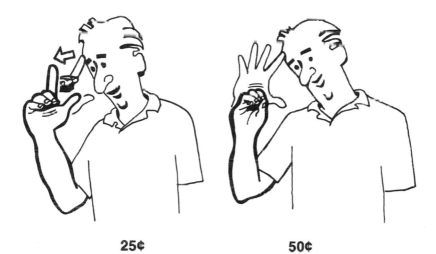

25¢   **50¢**

The same applies to these two signs as to the cent signs above.
Use them only when speaking of these amounts alone, and not
with a dollar amount.

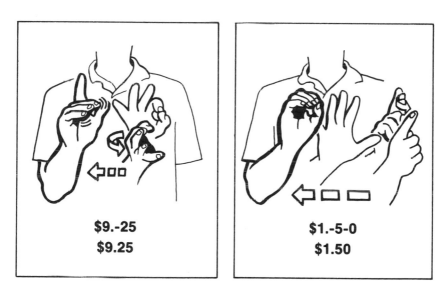

$9.-25   **$1.-5-0**
$9.25   **$1.50**

BOOK   COST   HOW MANY
How much does the book cost?

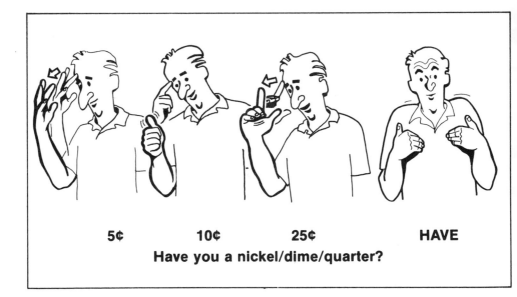

5¢   10¢   25¢   HAVE
Have you a nickel/dime/quarter?

$5.00   **SHARE (make change)**   **CAN**
Can you change a five?

PAY   **HOW MANY**
How much did you pay?

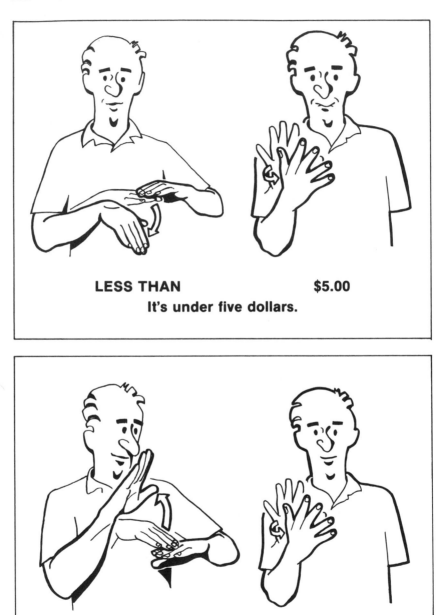

LESS THAN   **$5.00**
It's under five dollars.

MORE THAN   **$5.00**
It's over five dollars.

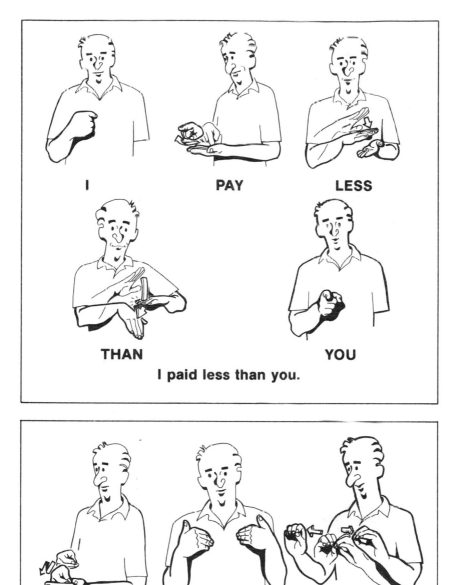

I   PAY   LESS

THAN   YOU

I paid less than you.

MONEY   HAVE   NONE

I have no money.

BROKE   **I**

I'm broke.

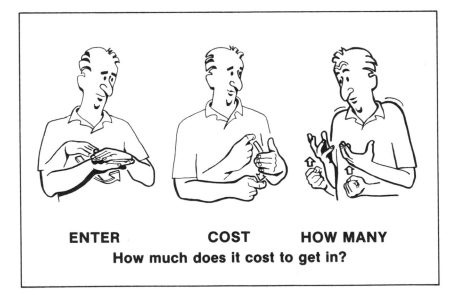

ENTER   COST   HOW MANY

How much does it cost to get in?

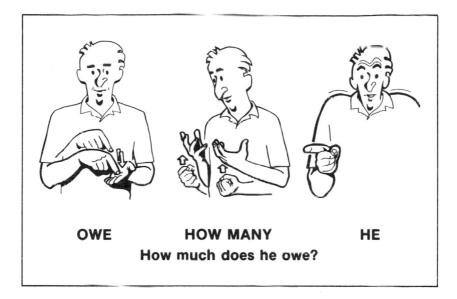

OWE **HOW MANY** **HE**
How much does he owe?

Appendix: The Manual Alphabet

The manual alphabet allows us to fingerspell English words. When there is not a sign for an idea, then fingerspelling is used. This occurs most often with proper names. Mastery of finger-spelling is relatively easy if you form good habits from the very beginning.

First, relax your fingers. This may require bending and stretch-ing the fingers so that they fall easily into the proper hand shapes. Next, relax your arm and shoulder. Tension is the greatest obsta-cle to clear formation of the letters, so strive to remain relaxed as you work at it. Let the arm hang down with the elbow to your side and the hand slightly in front of your body as the pictures show. Do not let your elbow start moving away from your side and rising upwards.

Rhythm is the most important quality to develop in fingerspel-ling. A rhythmical spelling is much easier to read than an unryth-mical one, even when the letters are not perfectly formed. Rhythm is also critical for indicating when one word has ended and the next word has begun. This is done by holding on to the last letter of a word for about one-fourth of a beat of the rhythm

336

you are using, then going on to the first letter of the next word. As you practice rhythmical fingerspelling, be sure you do not let the rhythm cause you to bounce your hand. Hold it steadily in one place.

Speed is not a goal to pursue. Work on rhythm, and then speed will come naturally in time. The tendency is to attempt to finger-spell too fast. Then the rhythm becomes broken when you cannot remember how to make a letter. A slow, rhythmic pattern is far more desirable than a fast but erratic rhythm.

Do not say the letters, either aloud or to yourself, as you make them. This is a very bad habit to get into and exceedingly hard to break once established. As you fingerspell a word, say the whole word. For instance, as you spell "C-A-T" do not say the letters, but say the word "cat." You may say it aloud or without voice. It will seem awkward at first, but you will quickly become used to it.

The reason for speaking the word rather than saying the letters has to do with lipreading. Deaf people are taught to lipread words, not letters. When you fingerspell they see both your hand and your lips, and the two complement and reinforce each other. (This is also the reason you do not let your fingerspelling hand wander out to your side, too far away from your face.) It is not necessary to speak the word aloud; you may mouth it without using your voice.

When fingerspelling long words, pronounce the word syllable by syllable as you fingerspell it. For example, say, "fin" as you fingerspell "F-I-N," then say "ger" as you fingerspell "G-E-R," and then say "spell" as you fingerspell "S-P-E-L-L." (Double letters are moved slightly to the side or humped back and forth slightly.) Caution: Do not pause after each syllable, but keep the rhythm flowing.

Practice spelling words, not just running through the alphabet. Begin with three-letter words, then work your way up to longer ones. A first-grade reading book provides excellent practice material because most of the words are short and are repeated often. Practice fingerspelling as you read a newspaper, listen to the radio or television, and see street signs and billboards. You may get some odd looks from some people, but never mind, you are on the road to mastering an intricate skill.

You will find that fingerspelling is much easier to do than to read. This happens because, initially, you tend to look for each individual letter as it is fingerspelled to you so that when you reach the end of the word you cannot make sense of the letters. You must learn to see whole words, not individual letters, just as you are doing as you read this printed material. You will have to find someone to learn and practice fingerspelling with you, since you cannot practice reading your own fingerspelling. As the two of you practice, do not speak or mouth the words since you would then hear or lipread them instead of reading the fingerspelling.

Here, in summary, are the tips to follow:

1. Relax.
2. Keep your elbow in and your hand in front of you.
3. Maintain a constant rhythm, but do not bounce your hand.
4. Pause for one-fourth of a beat at the end of each word.
5. Do not try to fingerspell rapidly.
6. Mouth or speak the word, not the letters.
7. Practice with someone so you can gain experience reading fingerspelling. (In this kind of practice, do not mouth or speak the word aloud.)
8. Look for the whole word, not individual letters.

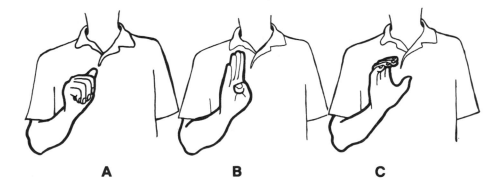

A   B   C

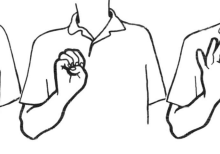

D **E** **F**

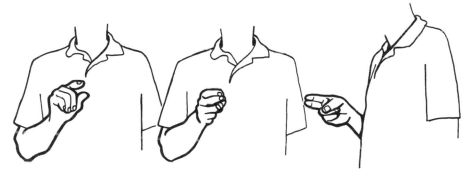

G **H** **H (side view)**

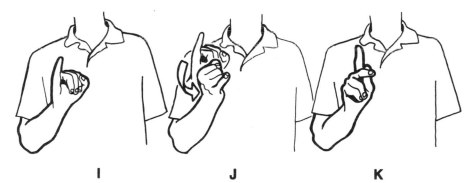

I **J** **K**

L   **M**   **N**

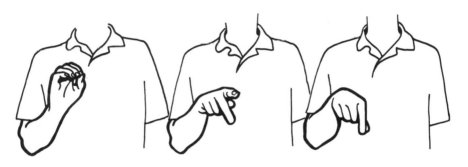

O*   **P**   **Q**

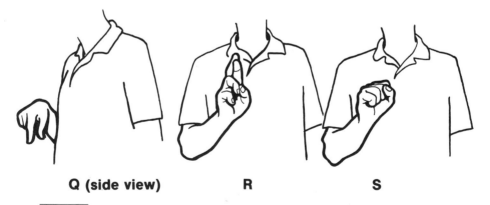

Q (side view)   **R**   **S**

*The sign for the letter "O" is the same as that for the number "0" (zero).

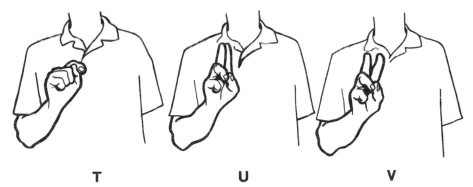

T   U   V

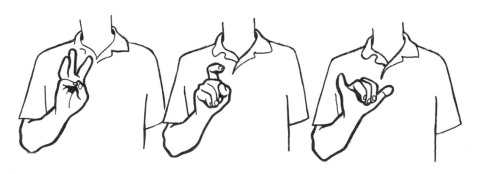

W   X   Y

Z

Dictionary/Index

The Dictionary/Index consists of a combination of three things:

1. All the signs in this book listed by sign labels. All sign labels are in capital letters. When the meaning of the sign is not evident from the sign label, additional definitions and explanations are given.

2. English words that are glossed by signs in this book. The word is printed in lower-case letters, and the correct sign is in all capitals within parentheses following the word. Example: food (EAT). It is suggested that you refer to the sign label in the Dictionary/Index to see if an additional definition or explanation is given before looking up the picture of the sign.

3. Topics that are discussed in various sections of this book. They are printed as titles. Examples: "Past, Present, Future"; "Labeling of the Drawings."

Abbreviations used:

SM = single movement. The movement of the sign is made only once.

DM = double movement. The movement of the sign is repeated once.

a lot of (MANY; MUCH), 132, 192

ability (SKILL), 157, 232

ABSENT, 190

ache (PAIN), 123, 126

acquire (GET), 286

ACT—actor/actress (also with the AGENT sign—optional); drama, play; theater, 113, 172

adapt (CHANGE), 251

address (LIVE), 108, 160

administer (CONTROL), 10, 178

advice (ADVISE), 173

ADVISE—counsel; guidance, advice; influence, 173

afraid (SCARE), 150

AFRICA, 240

AFTERNOON, 71, 149, 318

after a while (LATER), 78

AGAIN—SM: over again, repeat, 90; DM: over and over

AGAINST—opposed to, 283

against the law (PROHIBIT), 183, 262

age (OLD), 99, 118, 313

AGENT—A sign used in conjunction with another sign in order to designate a person who does a particular thing. Example: AIRPLANE AGENT = pilot. 104, 113, 158, 159, 163, 175, 200, 277, 284, 289, 290

ago (PAST), 14, 15, 30, 102, 133, 135, 145, 169, 230, 320

AGREE—concur; agreement; fitting, appropriate, becoming, 219

aid (HELP), 39

AIM—aspire, shoot for, hope to be; goal, objective, 158

AIRPLANE—SM: ride an airplane, fly, 51, 245; DM: airplane; airport, 163, 248, 250, 251, 252

AIRPLANE—LANDING, 60, 256

AIRPLANE—TAKE-OFF, 249, 251

ALL DAY, 318

all gone (USED UP), 127

ALL MORNING, 284

ALL NIGHT, 180, 262, 318

ALL RIGHT—be all right, be fine, be okay; it is all right; a civil right, 81, 119, 122

alike (SAME), 223

ALLIGATOR, 267

already (FINISH), 4, 6, 31, 133, 137, 151, 153, 164, 182, 189, 191, 202, 225, 245, 247, 254, 258, 275, 286, 293

alter (CHANGE), 252

although (BUT), 91, 230

ALWAYS, 218

ambulance (EMERGENCY VEHICLE), 135

AMERICA, 240

ANGEL, 298

Angle of the Pictures, 12

ANNUAL—every year, year after year, 317

ANIMAL—beast, creature, 267

Animals, 267–71

ANY, 131, 188

APPLE, 206

APPOINTMENT—reserve, reservation, engagement, 136, 253

appropriate (AGREE), 219

approve (SECOND MOTION), 285

April, 315
arid (DRY), 209
arise (GET UP), 301
ARIZONA, 266
arrange, arrangement (PLAN), 283
ARREST, 282
ARRIVE, 62, 257
ART—draw, 113, 172
Articles, 73
artist—combination of ART and AGENT, 112–14
AS—SM: as, like, same, 155; DM: also, accordingly
aspirin, 127
assist (HELP), 39
ask a question (QUERY), 182, 183, 188
ask for (PRAY), 300
aspire (AIM), 158
assembly (CONVENE), 169
atheist (DISBELIEVE), 292
ATLANTA, 246
attempt (TRY), 230
AUNT, 160, 320
AUSTRALIA, 240
AUTUMN, 149, 233, 319
away (ABSENT), 190
AWFUL—As an idiom it may mean: Terrific! Super! Awesome! 13, 187

BABY, 164
BACON, 206
baggage (LUGGAGE), 254
BANANA, 206
bankrupt (BROKE), 334
Baptist (BAPTIZE), 293
BAPTIZE, 13, 293, 294
BASEBALL, 226

BASKETBALL, 227
BATH—bathe, take a bath, 137, 259
bathroom (TOILET), 78
be able (CAN), 91, 98, 220, 229, 230, 261
BEAR, 268
beautiful (PRETTY), 142, 148
BECAUSE, 250, 282
BECKON, 265
BECOME—come to be, get to be, turn out to be; turn into, change into, 99
becoming (AGREE), 219
BED—go to bed, go to sleep; in bed, 131
BEE, 268
BEER, 198
before (PAST), 14, 15, 30, 102, 133, 135, 145, 169, 230, 320
begin (START), 185
BELIEVE, 298
BELT, 224, 255
BEST, 149
BET, 234
BETTER, 59, 130
big (LARGE), 57, 168, 279
BILLIARDS—pool, 227
BIRD, 268
BIRTH—give birth, 100, 109, 314, 315
birthday—combination of BIRTH and DAY, 315, 325
BLACK, 203, 272
BLESS, 298
BLIND, 105
blizzard, 153
BLOOD—bleed, 132
blouse (SHIRT), 219, 222, 223
BLOW NOSE—cold, have a cold, 124

BLUE, 219, 272
BODY, 131, 133, 173
Body Language, 27–29
BODY THERAPY (physical
    therapy)—combination of
    BODY and THERAPY, 173
BOIL, 210
bologna (SAUSAGE), 208
BOOK, 54, 72, 161, 162, 185, 330
boring (DRY), 209
born (BIRTH), 100
borrow (LEND), 139
BOTH, 204
BOW TIE, 221
BOWL, 238
BOY, 165, 166
BRAILLE, 105
BREAD, 211
BREAK, 131, 167, 190, 280
bright (CLEAR), 149
BRING—carry, take, 190, 248
BROKE—be out of money,
    bankrupt, 334
BROTHER, 156
BROWN, 272
BRUSH HAIR—brush one's hair;
    hairbrush, 140
build, 178
building (build), 178
bus, 257
business (BUSY), 172
BUSY—business, 172
BUT—although, however, still,
    yet; different, unlike; difference,
    91, 230
BUTTER, 211
BUTTERFLY, 268
button, 220
BUY—SM: buy, purchase, 56,
    128, 258, 320; DM: shopping,
    215

cab, 264
CABBAGE, 207
cafe (RESTAURANT), 193
CAKE, 212
CALIFORNIA, 266
call on the phone (PHONE), 85,
    264, 311
CAMEL, 268
camp (TENT), 230
CAN—be able; may; could;
    possible, 71, 91, 98, 220, 229,
    230
CANADA, 241
CANCEL, 251
CANOE—row, paddle; oar;
    rowboat, 231
CAN'T—be unable; may not;
    could not; not possible, 69, 91,
    181, 221, 224
cap (HAT), 224
capture (ARREST), 282
CAR—drive a car, 9, 21, 36, 56,
    81, 150, 260, 261, 282
CARDS—play cards; deal cards,
    227
CARROT, 207
CAT, 268
catch (ARREST), 282
CATSUP, 212
Cause and Effect Statements,
    58–59
cemetery (GRAVE), 299
certain, certainly (TRUE), 42
CHAIN—chains; the Olympics,
    150, 235
chair (SEAT), 86, 143, 253
CHANGE—adapt, alter, convert,
    modify, 252
chapter (LESSON), 12, 175
charge (COST), 278, 279, 330, 334
CHECKERS, 227

chemistry (SCIENCE), 172
CHERISH, 291
CHICAGO, 246, 252
CHICKEN—often the sign BIRD
  will mean "chicken," 207, 269
CHILDREN, 112, 118, 168
CHINA, 241
choir—combination of MUSIC
  and GROUP, 298
CHRIST, 290
CHRISTIAN—combination of
  CHRIST and AGENT, 290
CHRISTMAS, 324
CHURCH, 294, 295
cinema (MOVIE), 22, 44, 54, 65,
  70, 84, 102, 322
CITY—town, 160, 280
class (GROUP), 298
CLEANERS—dry cleaning,
  225
CLEAR—bright; light; obvious,
  71, 149, 273
CLOSE—shut, 79, 250
CLOSE BOOK, 184
CLOSE DOOR, 79
CLOSE WINDOW, 79
clothes (DRESS), 217
CLOUDS—cloudy; smoky; hazy,
  148
club, 101
COAT—put on an outer garment;
  coat, jacket, sweater, 146, 225
COCKTAIL—an alcoholic drink;
  have a drink, 194
COCONUT, 207
COFFEE, 9, 49, 202-4
COKE, 197
COLD—be cold; winter, 144, 149,
  150, 202, 319
cold (BLOW NOSE), 124

collect (CREAM), 203
COLLEGE—university, 103, 104,
  172
COLOR, 216
Colors, 272-73
COMB, 140
COME—used mainly to tell
  someone to approach, as in
  "Come on" and "Come here,"
  265
COME HERE, 168
come to be (BECOME), 99
command (ORDER), 194
committee (CONGRESS), 276,
  277
Commands or Requests, 54-55
COMMUNION—Holy
  Communion, used primarily
  among Roman Catholics, rarely
  among Protestants, 298
COMPETE—race; competition,
  contest, 6, 234, 235
COMPLAIN—object, protest;
  beef, gripe, grumble, 119
comprehend (UNDERSTAND),
  36, 92
COMPUTER, 174
concur (AGREE), 219
CONFESSION—a religious rite
  only, 298
conference (CONVENE), 169
confuse (MIX), 209
CONGRESS—committee, 276,
  277
congresswoman—combination of
  CONGRESS and WOMAN, 277
connect (JOIN), 287, 295
contest (COMPETE), 6, 234, 235
CONTROL—administer, direct,
  manage, run, 10, 178

CONVENE—meet in a group; assembly, convention, conference, 169

convention (CONVENE), 169

convert (CHANGE), 252

COOK—kitchen, stove, 206, 207

CORN, 208

COST—charge a fee, fine, penalize, tax; penalty; price; tax, 278, 279, 330, 334

could (CAN), 91, 98, 220, 229, 230, 261

could not (CAN'T), 91, 181, 221, 224

counsel (ADVISE), 173

COUNTRY—both "nation" and "rural area," 279

course (LESSON), 12, 175

course of study (MAJOR), 171

court (JUDGE), 286, 289

COUSIN, 163

COW, 269

CRACKER—also used for "Passover" because of the significance of matzo in the seder, 300

CRAZY—insane; nuts, loony, 234

CREAM—the dairy product; collect; earn, 203

creature (animal), 267

criticize (CANCEL), 251

CRUCIFY, 298, 299

crummy (LOUSY), 80, 200

cute (SWEET), 164

daily (EVERY DAY), 222, 228, 231, 318

DANCE, 236, 237

DARK, 273

dates, 313–27

DAUGHTER, 110, 159

DAY, 7, 142, 148, 221, 240, 315, 317

DEAF, 96, 99, 100, 104, 105

deal cards (CARDS), 227

debate (DISCUSS), 189

debt (OWE), 335

decimal, 310

DEER, 269

DELICIOUS, 7, 209

DEMOCRAT, 274

DENMARK, 241

DENTIST, 126

DEPART, 258

Descriptive Statements, 56–57

DESSERT, 212

DEVIL, 299

demand (REQUIRE), 150, 222

didn't (NOT), 14, 15, 47, 48, 50, 52, 96, 105, 122, 223, 253

DIE, 117, 135

difference (BUT), 91, 230

different (BUT), 91, 230

difficult (HARD), 210

diminishing (LESS), 333

dine (EAT), 14, 15, 47, 48, 191, 192, 202, 209, 214

direct (CONTROL), 10, 178

directionality, 35–40

DIRTY, 217

disappear (MELT), 151

DISBELIEVE—doubt, be skeptical; used often in such expressions as, "I doubt if he will come," 292

DISCUSS—talk about, talk over; debate, discussion, 189

DISGUST—offend, repel; disgusting, repulsive, sickening, 123

DISOBEY, 281

divide up (SHARE), 331

DIVORCE, 116

DO-DO—used to signify uncertainty about what to do, as in "Now what?," "What next?," and "What's to be done?" 236

DOCTOR, 112, 126

DOG, 269

DOLL, 167

DOLLAR, 327

DOMINOES, 227

don't (NOT) (DON'T), 14, 18, 68, 96, 105, 122, 223, 253

DON'T—used primarily to give a negative command, as in "Don't do that!" and "Don't tell!" 187

DON'T KNOW, 69

DON'T LIKE, 69, 232

DON'T WANT, 69

DOOR—The sign must be made so that the "door" is opened and then shut. If only one movement is used, it will mean "Open the door" or "Shut the door." 79

doubt (DISBELIEVE), 292

drama (ACT), 112, 172

draw (ART), 112, 172

DRAW BLOOD—take a sample of blood; donate blood, 132

DRESS—get dressed, put on clothes; clothes, dress, 216, 217, 218

drink (COCKTAIL), 194

drive a car (CAR), 21, 150, 261, 282

DRY—arid; boring, uninteresting, 209

dry cleaners (CLEANERS), 225

DURING—in the course of, at the time of; while; often expressed in English by the word "when," as in "When I was a boy . . . ," 150, 181, 183, 222, 233, 236

EAGLE, 269

earn (CREAM), 203

EARTH—geography, 153

earthquake—combination of EARTH and SHAKE, 153

EASY, 211

EAT—dine; food, 14, 15, 47, 48, 191, 192, 202, 209, 214

EDUCATION—This sign is used almost exclusively in academic circles. In most other situations, the TEACH sign is used., 172, 173

EGG, 209–211

eggs over easy—combination of FLIP OVER and EASY, 211

EGYPT, 241

elect (VOTE), 275, 276

ELECTRONIC GAMES—This is a new sign and thus may not be known by many deaf people, 227

ELEPHANT, 269

ELEVATOR, 260

EMERGENCY VEHICLE— ambulance or any emergency vehicle, 135

enemy (OPPOSITE), 219

ENGLISH—stands for both the country of England and the language, 171, 241

enjoy (PLEASE), 101, 143, 229, 257

ENOUGH, 205
ENTER, 104, 334
EPISCOPAL, 293
ERASE BOARD, 187
et cetera (VARIOUS), 198
EUROPE, 241
EVERY DAY, 222, 228, 231, 318
EVERY SATURDAY, 322
EVERY SUNDAY, 294
EVERY THREE MONTHS, 321
EVERY TUESDAY, 322
every year (ANNUAL), 317
evening (NIGHT), 214
exam (TEST), 183, 184
except, exception (SPECIAL), 173
excessive (TOO MUCH), 206, 282
Exclamatory Statements, 55
EXCUSE—pardon, 83, 190
EXERCISE, 235
expect (HOPE), 149, 235
experience a thing (TOUCH), 245

FACE—resemble, look like, 154, 155
Facial Expressions, 15, 24 27
FAIL, 188
FAITH—trust, 299
FAMILY, 168, 169
FARM, 61, 159, 169
fast (RAPID), 92, 282
FATHER, 21, 100, 135, 154, 166
fatigue (TIRED), 80
fee (COST), 278, 279, 330, 334
FEEL—sense, 59, 80, 121, 122, 130
FEW—several, 157
film (MOVIE), 22, 54, 84, 102, 322
filthy (DIRTY), 217
FINE—all right, okay, 80
fine (COST), 279

FINGERSPELL—spell, 91, 94
FINISH—(1) done with, over with; (2) when used with a verb sign, places the action of the verb in the past; example; EAT FINISH means "ate," "eaten," "did eat," etc., 4, 31, 59, 62, 66, 67, 133, 137, 151, 153, 164, 182, 189, 191, 245, 247, 254, 258, 275, 286, 293 (3) often covers the meaning of "when," "after," and "then," as in "When he had eaten he left," and "He ate, then he left," all of which are signed: EAT FINISH HE DEPART, 5, 202, 225 (4) used idiomatically to mean, "That's enough!," "Stop it!," "Don't do that!" 6
FINLAND, 241
FIREFIGHTER, 113
FIRST, 103
FISH, 207
FISHING, 229
The Five Aids for Reading the Drawings, 7
FLIP OVER, 211
FLOOD, 152
FLOWER, 41
FLUNK, 188
FOLLOW, 37
food (EAT), 209
FOOTBALL, 8, 227
FOR, 129, 278
forbid (PROHIBIT), 120, 183, 262
FORK, 212
Fractions, 309
FRANCE, 242
free (SAVE), 301
free time (VACATION), 323
freeze (ICE), 144

FRESHMAN, 176
FRIDAY, 316
FRIEND, 110
frighten (SCARE), 150
FROM, 269
FROM, 108
FUNERAL, 299
future (WILL), 72, 161, 281

GALLAUDET—Thomas H.
    Gallaudet; Gallaudet College.
    This is also the sign for glasses
    (spectacles), 103, 104
GALOSHES—overshoes, 147
geography (earth), 153
GERMANY—German, 242
GET—acquire, obtain; receive,
    286
get dressed (DRESS), 216, 218
get in (GET ON), 254
GET ON, 254
get to a place (ARRIVE), 257
get to be (BECOME), 99
GET UP—arose from a sitting or
    prone position, 301
ghost (SOUL), 301
GIRAFFE, 269
GIRL, 165, 167
GIVE, 189
GIVE ME, 54, 161, 189
glad (HAPPY), 8, 77
glasses, spectacles
    (GALLAUDET), 103, 104
GO—The emphasis is on leaving,
    departing, going away. 87
go away—(1) DEPART, 258; (2)
    GO, 87; (3) MELT, 151
GO TO—The emphasis is on
    arriving, going to a place. 5,
    22, 44, 50, 51, 65, 69, 84, 102,
    179, 193, 215, 229, 240, 259,
    286, 289, 294, 295, 322

go to sleep (BED), 131
go into (ENTER), 104, 334
goal (AIM), 158
GOAT, 270
GOD, 299
GOING—The emphasis is the act
    itself as it is happening. If you
    and a deaf person are walking
    along together and you wish to
    ask where you are going, use
    this sign. It is used less often
    than the other signs for "go." 9,
    88
GOLF, 227
gone (1) ABSENT, 190 (2) GO, 87
good—THANK YOU, 46, 75, 76,
    82, 83, 91, 122, 289
good-bye, 78
GOT TO (MUST), 87, 94, 128,
    129, 130, 132, 179, 190, 215,
    217, 223, 252, 278, 279, 281,
    289
GOVERNMENT, 277, 278, 280
governor—combination of
    GOVERNMENT and AGENT,
    277
GRAB—take, 224
grab (ARREST), 282
GRADUATE, 176, 127, 321
graduate school—combination of
    GRADUATE and SCHOOL,
    177
graduate student—combination of
    GRADUATE, LEARN, and
    AGENT, 175–76
GRANDFATHER, 162, 169
GRANDMOTHER, 162
GRAVE—tomb; cemetery, 299
gravy (GREASE), 212
GRAY, 272
GREASE—oily; gravy, 212
GREECE—Greek, 242

GREEN, 272
gripe (COMPLAIN), 119
GROUP—class, 298
GROW—spring, 41, 149, 318
grumble (COMPLAIN), 119
guidance (ADVISE), 173

hail, 153
HAIR DRYER, 139
hairbrush (BRUSH HAIR), 140
HAMBURGER, 10, 199
HANDBALL, 227
HANUKKAH, 324
HAPPY—glad; merry, 8, 60, 77,
   107, 324, 325
HARD, 210
HARD OF HEARING, 92
hard-boiled eggs, 210
HAT—cap, 224
HATE, 235
HAVE—own, possess, 81, 85, 94,
   117, 118, 120, 127, 141, 146,
   198, 217, 231, 249, 260, 261,
   323, 330
have to (MUST), 87, 94, 128, 129,
   130, 132, 179, 190, 215, 217,
   223, 252, 278, 279, 281, 289
HAWAII, 242, 266
HAWK, 270
HE/HIM/SHE/HER/IT, 20, 21,
   36, 37, 54, 68, 165, 192, 199,
   218, 231, 232, 234, 235, 277,
   282, 287, 288, 292, 296, 313,
   322, 335
HEADACHE, 125
HEALTH—This is a new sign so
   it may not be known by many
   deaf people. It is used mostly in
   academic circles. 173
HEAR, 99

HEARING AID, 97
HEAVEN, 299
Hebrew (JEWISH), 291, 295
HE GIVES HER, 162
HELL, 299
HELLO, 74
HELP—aid, assist, 39
HERE, 159, 262
HIMSELF/HERSELF/ITSELF,
   64
HIS/HER/ITS, 63, 158, 159, 161,
   162, 167
HISTORY, 172
HOLLAND—Dutch, 242
HOME, 5, 87
home economics— combination of
   HOME and E-C-O, 174
HOPE—expect, 71, 149, 235
hope to be (AIM), 158
hope for (AIM), 71, 158
HORSE, 234, 270
HOSPITAL, 134, 141
HOT, 143, 202
HOTEL, 62, 259
hour (ONE HOUR), 251
HOUSE, 57, 61, 114, 320
housewife—combination of
   HOUSE and WIFE, 114
HOW, 46, 76, 77, 93, 99, 121, 259,
   262
HOW MANY—how much, 168,
   330, 331, 334, 335
how much (HOW MANY), 99,
   118, 330, 334
HUNGER—wish; desire; passion,
   lust, 44, 193
hunt for (SEARCH), 133
HUNTING, 233
hurricane, 153
hurt (PAIN), 123
HUSBAND, 110, 112, 134
HYPODERMIC—get a shot, 130

I/ME, 20, 30, 31, 32, 33, 34, 35,
    36, 37, 42, 50, 51, 53, 58, 59,
    60, 62, 65, 67, 68, 70, 86, 89,
    103, 107, 112, 116, 149, 156,
    172, 178, 181, 196, 199, 228,
    230, 238, 240, 248, 275, 279,
    284, 314, 321, 333, 334
ICE—freeze, 144
ICE CREAM, 212
ICE SKATE, 230
ill (SICK), 42
illegal (PROHIBIT), 262
impossible (CAN'T), 91, 181, 221,
    224
IN—inside; within, 61, 104, 252
INDEPENDENT, 274
INDIA, 242
influence (ADVISE), 173
inform (NOTIFY), 286
insane (CRAZY), 234
INSECT, 270
inside (IN), 104, 252
INSTITUTION—Although this
    sign means "institution," it is
    used almost exclusively to mean
    a residential school for deaf
    children. 102
instruct (TEACH), 114, 183
INSURANCE, 141
intend—(MEAN), 95
INTERPRET, 297
INTRODUCE, 109
IRELAND—Irish, 242
ISRAEL—Israeli, 243
IT—he; she, 20, 21, 35, 36, 37, 45,
    68, 165, 192, 199, 218, 231, 232,
    234, 235, 277, 282, 287, 288,
    292, 296, 313, 322, 335
ITALY—Italian, 243
ITS—his; her, 63, 158, 159, 161,
    162, 167
ITSELF—himself; herself, 54

jacket (COAT), 146, 225
JAIL—prison, 280
JAPAN—Japanese, 243, 245
JESUS, 300
JEWISH—Hebrew, 291, 295
job (WORK), 5
JOIN—connect, 287, 295
journal (MAGAZINE), 255
July, 323
JUNIOR, 176
JUDGE—court; trial, 277, 286,
    289
judge—combination of JUDGE
    and AGENT, 277

KNEEL, 292
KNIFE, 212
KNOW, 53, 69, 262

Labeling of the Drawings, 13–14
LANGUAGE, 89, 157
LAST WEEK—a week ago, 316
LAST YEAR—a year ago, 152,
    177, 284, 317
LARGE—big, 57, 168, 279
LATE—In addition to meaning
    tardy, this sign is used a great
    deal to mean "not yet." It
    implies that an event has not
    taken place, but will take place.
    For example, the sentence EAT
    LATE means, "I haven't eaten
    yet." 41, 139, 189, 192
LATE AFTERNOON, 148
LATER—after awhile, 78
laundromat (WASHING
    MACHINE), 218
laundry (WASHING MACHINE),
    217
LAW, 112, 276, 277, 280, 281, 289
lawyer—combination of LAW and
    AGENT, 113–14, 277, 289

LEARN, 89, 104, 175, 237, 284
leave (DEPART), 258
LEFT—opposite of right, 263
LEFT TURN, 263
LEGISLATURE, 276
LEMON, 207
LEND—borrow, 139, 181
LESS—diminishing, growing less, 333
LESS THAN, 152, 332
LESSON—course; chapter, 12, 175
LET'S SEE—used in expressions such as "We'll see about that," 250
LETTUCE, 207
liberate (SAVE), 301
LIBRARY, 178
LICENSE, 261
LIE DOWN, 131
light (CLEAR), 273
LIGHTNING, 58, 145
Light, Sight and Space, 17–23
LIKE—be attracted to, enjoy, 54, 65, 69, 84, 149, 178, 199, 226, 236
like (AS), 155
line of work (MAJOR), 111
LION, 270
LIPREAD— Schools for deaf children that do not use any sign language in their instructional program are called "oral" schools. This sign is used to refer to these schools. A school for hearing children is signed SPEAK SCHOOL. The LIPREAD sign also means "speech" and "to read lips." 71, 98
LITTLE BIT—not much, 98
LIVE—life; address, 57, 108, 160

LOAF, 236
LOBSTER, 208
loiter (LOAF), 236
LONG—used only in the sense of a long span of something that endures or lasts for a long time, 82, 259
LONG AGO—used a great deal to convey the idea of "used to," as in "We used to see him every day," 296
LOOK—watch; stare, 65, 84
look like (FACE), 154, 155
loony (CRAZY), 234
LORD, 300
LOSE, 99, 132, 140, 147, 186
LOUSY—awful, terrible, rotten, crummy, 80, 200
LOVE, 35, 165, 234
lovely (PRETTY), 142, 148
LUGGAGE—baggage; suitcase, 254
LUTHERAN, 293

MAGAZINE—journal, 255
magnificent (WONDERFUL), 81
MAJOR—course of study in school; line of work; specialty, 111, 171
make change (SHARE), 331
Making Statements, 43
MAN, 61, 163
manage (CONTROL), 10, 178
Manual Alphabet, 336–41
MANY—a lot of, 104, 233
MARRY, 115
MASS—the religious ritual only, 300
MATCH, 120
MATH, 172
may (CAN), 91, 98, 220, 229, 230, 261

may not (CAN'T), 91, 181, 221, 224

MAYBE—perhaps; possibly, 145, 280

ME/I, 20, 37, 38, 52, 53, 56, 57, 58, 59, 150, 161, 297

meal (EAT), 209, 214

MEAN—intend; intention, meaning, 95

MEAT, 205

MEDICINE, 59, 127, 128

MEDIUM (glass), 201

MEET—encounter another person, 107, 256

MELT—disappear, go away, 151

MELON, 208

mercy (PITY), 300

merry (HAPPY), 8, 324

MEXICO—Mexican, 243

MILK, 201, 203

MILWAUKEE, 246

MINUTE, 201, 256

missing (ABSENT), 190

modify (CHANGE), 252

MISSIONARY, 296

MIX—confuse, 209

MONDAY, 316, 319

Money, 326–38

MONTH, 135, 317

MONTHLY, 317

MONKEY, 270

MORE THAN, 332

MORNING, 31, 75, 144, 318

MORMON, 293

MOST, 221

MOTHER, 36, 100, 155

MOUNTAIN, 150, 229

MOUSE, 270

MOVIE—cinema, film, motion pictures, 22, 44, 54, 65, 84, 102, 322

MUCH—a lot, 132

MULE, 270

MUSEUM—This is a new sign that many deaf people will not know, but it is gaining wide acceptance rapidly. 22

MUSIC—sing, song, 172, 298

MUST—SM: necessary, have to, go to, obligated to. The idea here is that one has no choice. 94, 252, 278, 279, 281; DM: should, ought to. The idea here is that it would be a good idea, but that it is not obligatory. The double movement may also mean "need." 87, 128, 129, 130, 132, 179, 190, 215, 217, 223, 289

MY—mine, 63, 136, 156, 157, 159, 160, 163, 180, 181, 220, 224, 311, 315

MYSELF, 64

NAME, 106, 107, 248, 280

Names and Titles, 73

NEAR, 218

NEAR FUTURE—used mostly to refer to days of the week that are coming up within the coming week, 319

necessary (MUST), 126

need, need to (MUST), 126, 130

Negation, 68–69

Negative Questions, 51–52

NEPHEW, 161

NEVER, 8, 72, 199, 230

NEW, 21, 56, 275, 320

NEW ORLEANS, 246

NEW YORK, 62, 245, 266

NEWSPAPER, 255

NEXT WEEK—a week from now, 33, 317

NEXT YEAR—a year from now, 317

NICE—**SM**: nice, clean, neat, 154, 218, 323; **DM**: clean up, tidy up,

NIECE, 161

NIGHT—evening, 14, 15, 30, 33, 47, 48, 72, 102, 144, 145, 214, 216, 245, 318

NONE—not any; nothing; no one, 60, 68, 94, 261

NOON, 214, 318

NORWAY— Norwegian, 243

NOT—don't; didn't, 14, 15, 47, 48, 50, 52, 68, 96, 105, 122, 223, 253

not allowed (PROHIBIT), 120, 183, 262

not any (NONE), 68, 82, 94, 261

not much (LITTLE BIT), 98

not yet (LATE), 139, 189, 192

nothing (NONE), 68

NOTIFY—inform, 286

NOW—at present, 33, 71, 130, 142, 144, 148, 149, 175, 177, 216, 221, 237, 245, 254

NUMBER, 85, 302, 311

Numbers, 302–11

NUT, 208

nuts (CRAZY), 234

oar (CANOE), 231

OBEY, 281

object (COMPLAIN), 119

objective (AIM), 158

obtain (GET), 286

obvious (CLEAR), 149

ocean, (WATER, WAVE [1], WAVE [2], WAVE [3]), 232

ODD—strange, queer, 216

offend, offensive, (DISGUST), 123

oily (GREASE), 212

okay (1) ALL RIGHT, 81, 119, 122 (2) FINE, 80

OLD—age, 57, 61, 99, 118, 291, 313

Olympics (CHAIN), 235

ONE HOUR, 251

one-half sign, 309

ONION, 208

ONLY—single, alone. In addition to this meaning, the ONLY sign means "some" in expressions such as "someone," "someday," "something," and "somehow," either in combination with the signs ONE, DAY, THING, and HOW, or all by itself. In the sentence, "I had some feeling that everything was not right," the ONLY sign is used for the idea of "some." 116, 204, 240, 264

OPEN BOOK, 185

OPEN DOOR, 79

OPEN WINDOW, 79

operation (SURGERY), 134

opponent (OPPOSITE), 134

opposed (AGAINST), 283

OPPOSITE—enemy, opponent, 219

ORAL THERMOMETER, 129

organize (PLAN), 283

ORANGE, 208, 273

ORDER—command, 194

ought (MUST), 87, 94, 128, 129, 130, 132, 179, 190, 215, 217, 223, 252, 278, 279, 281, 289

out of money (BROKE), 334

outside (OUT), 166

OUR, 63, 168, 279

OURSELVES, 64

OUT—outside, 166

over easy (eggs)—combination of
FLIP OVER and EASY, 211
OWE—debt, 335
overshoes (GALOSHES), 147
own (HAVE), 81, 85, 117, 118,
120, 127, 141, 146, 198, 217,
231, 249, 260, 261, 330

PACK BAGS, 247
paddle (CANOE), 231
PAIN, 60, 123
PANTS—trousers, 220
PAPER, 179, 189
pardon (EXCUSE), 83, 190
park (VEHICLE), 262, 279
PASS, 188, 276, 285
Passover (CRACKER), 300
PAST—This sign is often
interchangeable with the
FINISH sign to indicate that an
action is in the past. The
sentence MOVIE SEE PAST
means, "I've seen this movie
before," which is essentially the
same as, "I've already seen the
movie." 14, 15, 30, 32, 47, 48,
102, 133, 135, 145, 169, 230
Past, Present, Future, 29–34
PAY, 278, 279, 321, 333
pen, pencil (WRITE), 186
penalize, penalty (COST), 279
PENSION, 287, 288
PEOPLE, 60, 105, 233
PEPPER, 12
PEPSI, 197
percent, 309
perhaps (MAYBE), 145, 280
PETITION—suggest, suggestion,
285
PHILADELPHIA, 246
PHONE, 85, 264, 311
PHILOSOPHY, 173

phrase (SENTENCE), 101, 102
physical therapy—combination of
BODY and THERAPY, 173
PHYSICIAN—doctor, 112, 126
PICKET, 284
PICKLE—sour, 208
PIE, 213
PINK, 273
PILL, 59, 128
PITTSBURGH, 246
PITY—mercy, 300
Placement of Signs, 20–23
PLAN—organize, prepare, 283
PLAY—to play games, 166, 226
play (ACT), 112
play cards (CARDS), 227
PLEASE—enjoy; pleasure. Also
used for politeness in requests
such as "Please sit down." 57,
83, 86, 90, 93, 101, 143, 187,
203, 204, 229, 257, 264
pleasure (PLEASE), 83, 101, 143,
229, 264
Plurals, 72
POCKET CALCULATOR, 180
POLAND, 244
POLICE, 114, 282
pool (BILLIARDS), 227
possess (HAVE), 81, 85, 117, 118,
120, 127, 141, 146, 198, 217,
231, 249, 260, 261, 330
possible (CAN), 91, 98, 220, 229,
230, 261
possibly (MAYBE), 145, 280
POSTPONE—put off, 251
POTATO, 208
PRAY—ask for, request, 300
PREACH—sermon, 296, 297
predict (PROPHECY), 300
prep student—combination of
PREP, LEARN, and AGENT,
175–76

prepare (PLAN), 283
present, presently (NOW), 33, 130, 142, 144, 148, 149, 175, 177, 216, 221, 237, 245, 254
PRESIDENT—superintendent, 275
PRETTY—beautiful, lovely, 142, 148
price (COST), 278, 279, 330, 334
PRIEST, 300
prison (JAIL), 280
PROHIBIT—against the law, forbidden, illegal, not allowed, 120, 183, 262
Pronouns, 63–67
PROPHECY—predict, 300
PROTEST—strike, 283, 284
protest (COMPLAIN), 119
protestant (KNEEL), 292
PSYCHOLOGY, 172
P.T.A., 287
PULL TOOTH, 133
PUNISH, 281
PURPLE, 273
PUT, 225

queer (ODD), 216
QUERY—ask a question, inquire, 182, 183, 188
quiz (TEST), 183, 184

RABBI, 301
RABBIT, 270, 271
RAIN, 40, 50, 146
RAPID—fast, 92, 282
RAT, 271
reach a place (ARRIVE), 257
READ, 91
Reading the Drawings, 7–11
READY, 254
real, really (TRUE), 42
receive (GET), 286

RED, 56, 195, 273
regret (SORRY), 88
relax (REST), 237
RELIGION, 291
repeat (AGAIN), 90
REPUBLICAN, 274
repulsive (DISGUST), 123
request (PRAY), 300
REQUIRE—demand, 150, 222
RESEARCH, 179
resemble (FACE), 155
reserve, reservation (APPOINTMENT), 136, 253
RESPONSIBLE, 276
REST—relax, 237
rest room (TOILET), 78
RESTAURANT—cafe, 193
resurrection—combination of GET UP and AGAIN, 301
Rhetorical Questions (RHQ), 50
RIDE HORSE, 234
RIGHT—the opposite of left, 263
right (ALL RIGHT), 81, 119, 122
RIGHT TURN, 263
RIP—tear, 220
ROCKET, 158
ROLLER SKATE, 230
ROMAN CATHOLIC, 292
ROOMMATE, 181
rotten, (LOUSY), 80, 200
row boat (CANOE), 231
RUBBER, 147
RUN, 3, 228
run against; run for office (COMPETE), 6
RUNNY NOSE, 124
RUSSIA, 244

SAILBOAT—sailing, 231
SALAD, 213
SALT, 213
salvation (SAVE), 301

SAME—similar, 223
SAN FRANCISCO, 247
SANDWICH, 199
SATURDAY, 295, 316
SAUSAGE—bologna, 208
SAVE—free, liberate; safe,
    salvation, 60, 301
say (SPEAK), 96, 98, 103
SCARE—afraid; frighten, 58, 150
SCHOOL, 103, 115, 170, 177
SCIENCE—chemistry, 172
SCOTLAND—Scottish, Scot;
    Scotch (the drink), 196, 244
scrambled eggs—combination of
    EGG and MIX, 209
SEARCH—hunt for, 133
seat (SIT), 86, 143, 253
SECOND MOTION—approve,
    285
SECRETARY, 114
SEE, 21, 29, 30, 31, 32, 33, 34, 37,
    38, 77, 78, 82, 102, 164, 319,
    322
SEMESTER, 175
SENATE, 277
senator—combination of SENATE
    and AGENT, 277
SENIOR, 176
sense (FEEL), 80, 121, 122, 130
SENTENCE—phrase, 101, 102
sermon (PREACH), 297
SERVE—wait on, 200
several (FEW), 157
SEW, 220
SHAKE—thunder, 58, 153
shall (WILL), 34, 161, 281
SHARE—divide up; make
    change, 331
SHAVE, 139
SHE HELP YOU, 161

SHEEP, 271
SHIFT GEARS, 262
SHIRT—blouse, 219, 222, 223
SHOE, 222
shopping (BUY), 215
SHORTER SLEEVE, 225
SHORT—height, 166, 167
SHORTS, 222
should (MUST), 87, 94, 128, 129,
    130, 132, 179, 190, 215, 217,
    223, 252, 278, 279, 281, 289
SHOWER, 137
shut (CLOSE), 79, 250
SICK—ill, 42
sickening (DISGUST), 123
The Sight Line, 18–23
SIGN—sign language, 89, 90, 92,
    93, 94
Sign Labels, 3–6
similar (SAME), 223
Simple Statements, 52–54
SIN, 301
sing (MUSIC), 172
since (1) BECAUSE, 250, 282; (2)
    UP TILL NOW, 77, 82, 131
SISTER, 157
SIT—chair, seat; have a seat, 86,
    143, 253
skeptic, skeptical (DISBELIEVE),
    292
SKI, 229
SKILL—ability, talent, 157, 232
SLACKS, 221
SLEEP, 181
sleet, 153
SLOW, 90, 263
SMALL, 168
SMALL (glass), 201
SMOKE CIGARETTE, 119, 120
smoky (CLOUD), 148

SNAKE, 271
SNOW, 145, 151
SOCCER, 228
Social Security (S.S.), 287
SOCKS, 223
SOFT, 210
soft-boiled eggs, 210
SOFT DRINK, 198
Some Dos and Don'ts, 16
someone, something (ONLY), 240, 264
SON, 110, 158
song (MUSIC), 172
SOPHOMORE, 176
SORRY—regret, 88
SOUL—ghost, spirit, 301
sour (PICKLE), 208
SPAIN—Spanish, 244
SPEAK—say, speech, 96, 98, 103
SPECIAL—except, exception, exceptional, 173
Special Education—combination of SPECIAL and EDUCATION, 173
specialty (MAJOR), 111, 171
speech (SPEAK), 96, 98, 103
spell (FINGERSPELL), 91, 94
spirit (SOUL), 301
SPOON, 213
spring (GROW), 149, 318
stare (LOOK), 65, 84
START—begin, 185
Statements That Ask Questions, 44–52
Statements That Do Not Ask Questions, 52–55
Statements That Move from the General to the Specific, 61–62
Statements That Require Real-Time Sequencing, 59–60

STAY HERE, 259
Stimulus-Response Statements, 58–59
STINGY, 291
STOMACHACHE, 126
STOP, 186, 237, 263
stove (COOK), 205, 206
strange (ODD), 216
strike (PROTEST), 283
Stringing the Signs Together, 55
STUCK, 260
student—combination of LEARN and AGENT, 104, 175, 284
STUDY, 178
sue, bring suit against (AGAINST), 283
suitcase (LUGGAGE), 254
sugar (SWEET), 203, 204
suggest, suggestion (PETITION), 285
SUMMER, 149, 169, 222, 230, 318
summon (BECKON), 135, 264
SUN, 143
SUN RAY, 143
Sunday (WONDERFUL), 316
sunny side up (eggs)—THUMB UP, 210
SUNSET, 148
superintendent (PRESIDENT), 275
Supplementary Salary Income (S.S.I.), 288
SUPPORT, 278
sure, surely (TRUE), 42, 57
SURFBOARD, 232
SURGERY—operation, 134
sweater (COAT), 146, 225
SWEDEN, 244
SWEET—cute; sugar, 164, 203, 204
SWIM, 232

TABLE TENNIS, 228
take (1) BRING, 190, 248; (2) GRAB, 224
TAKE UP—as in "to take Spanish" or "take up golf," 175
talent (SKILL), 157, 232
TALK, 157, 183
talk about, talk over (DISCUSS), 189
TALL (glass), 197, 201
tasty (DELICIOUS), 7, 209
tax (COST), 278
TDD, 85, 310
TEA, 49, 202
TEACH—instruct, 112, 183
teacher—combination of TEACH and AGENT, 114
tear (RIP), 220
telephone (PHONE), 85, 264, 311
TELL, 37, 52, 53, 66, 67, 68, 72, 165, 166
TELL ME, 68
TEMPERATURE—thermometer, 129, 151, 152
TEMPLE, 295
TENNIS, 228
terrible (1) AWFUL, 13, 187; (2) LOUSY, 80, 200
TENT—camp, camping, 230
TEST—quiz, exam, 183, 184
TEXAS, 266
THAN, 156, 333
thank you (GOOD), 82, 83
THANKSGIVING, 307
THAT—This sign can mean: this, that, them, those, they, and it. Idiomatically it can mean: "Oh, I see," "So, that's it," or "Ah, ha, I get it!" It is often done by the watcher while the signer is signing, in much the same way hearing people nod their head and say "uh-huh" or "yes" while listening to the speaker. 163
theater (ACT), 112, 172
THEIR, 64
THEMSELVES, 64
THERAPY—This is a new sign used mostly in academic circles, but it is gaining fast acceptance. 173
THERE, 57, 61, 62, 160, 169
thermometer (TEMPERATURE), 129, 151, 152
THEY—them, 64, 283
THUMB UP, 210
thunder (SHAKE), 58, 145
THURSDAY, 316
TICKET, 249, 250, 254, 258
TIE, 219
TIE KNOT, 221
TIGER, 271
Time, 312–13
TIME—the time of day as well as "time" in "three times" and "have a good time," 82, 87, 129, 136, 249, 257, 258, 265, 312, 313
TIRED—weary, 62
TOAST, 213
To Be or Not to Be, 40–43
together (WITH), 86
TOILET—bathroom, rest room, 78
TOMATO, 208
tomb (GRAVE), 299
TOMORROW, 32, 70, 145, 184
TOO MUCH—excess, excessive, overdo; too, too many, 192, 206, 282
TOOTHACHE, 125

TOOTHBRUSH—brush one's teeth, 136, 137

Topic-Comment Statements, 55–63

TORNADO, 150

TOUCH—to experience a thing, 245

town (CITY), 160, 280

TRAIN, 41, 257, 258

TREE, 11, 72

TRUE—certain, certainly, indeed, real, really, sure, surely, truly, truth; used mainly to give emphasis to a state of being or condition, 42, 57

truth (TRUE), 42, 57

TRY—attempt, 230

TTY, 85, 310

TUESDAY, 316

TURKEY, 271

turn into (BECOME), 99

T.V., 65, 84, 101

TWO HOURS, 253

TWO MONTHS, 320

TWO YEARS AGO, 320

TWO YEARS FROM NOW, 321

TYPEWRITER, 181

UMBRELLA, 147

UNCLE, 159

UNDERSTAND—comprehend, 36, 92

university (COLLEGE), 103, 171

UNTIL, 313

UP TILL NOW—to express the idea that an event has/has not been going on from some time in the past up until now, or up until very recently. It stands for the idea of "since" in "I haven't seen you since last Tuesday"

and of "been" in "I've been sick for the last month." 77, 82, 131

USE, 97, 221

used to (LONG AGO), 296

USED UP—all gone, 127

VACATION—free time, 323

variety (VARIOUS), 198

vegetable, 206

VEHICLE—park vehicle; can stand for any type conveyance (car, bus, train, airplane, motorcycle, bike, etc.), 262, 279

Verb Directionality, 35–40

VISIT—This sign, combined with the AGENT sign, makes "guest." 101, 265, 320

VOLLEYBALL, 228

VOTE—elect, 275, 276

WAIT—wait for, 11, 201, 253

wait on (SERVE), 200

WANT, 12, 36, 44, 49, 65, 69, 70, 84, 101, 137, 194, 195, 196, 197, 198, 201, 202, 203, 237, 255, 297

WASH CLOTHES, 223

WASH FACE, 138

WASH HANDS, 138

WASHING MACHINE—laundromat, 217, 218

WASHINGTON—both the city and the state, as well as George, 104, 247, 266

watch (LOOK), 65, 84

WATER, 152, 196, 232

WAVE, 232

WE—for more than two persons, 169, 231, 278

WE TWO, 189

weary (TIRED), 62, 80
WEDNESDAY, 316
WEEK, 316
WEEK AGO, 133
WEEKLY, 238, 317
WET—moist, 209
Wh- Sign Questions, 45–49
WHAT, 45, 311
WHAT SHRUG—This sign and the WHAT sign are essentially the same, but the WHAT SHRUG sign is used much more. 45, 85, 95, 111, 151, 175, 194, 216, 236, 280
WHEN, 46 (The DURING sign is used in sentences like "When I was a boy . . ." when no question is being asked.)
WHERE, 46, 78, 88, 108, 109, 111, 123, 136, 147, 178, 180, 200
WHICH, 9, 46, 49, 188, 248, 292, 295
while (DURING), 181
WHISKEY, 199
WHITE, 61, 195, 273
WHO, 45, 163, 224, 275, 276
WHY, 14, 15, 45, 47, 48, 50, 52
WIFE, 109, 114, 117, 134
WILL—Although this sign does refer to the future ("shall"), it is used much more to express intention. 34, 72, 161, 281
WIN, 276
WIND, 148
WINDOW—The sign must be made so that the "window" is opened then shut. If only one movement is used, it will mean "Open the window" or "Shut the window." 79

WINE, 195
winter (COLD), 149, 150, 319
wish (HUNGER), 193
WITH—together, 86
within (IN), 104, 252
WOMAN, 164, 221, 277
WONDERFUL—Sunday, 81, 316
Words versus Signs, 43
WORK—job, 5, 111, 159
WORM, 271
WORSHIP, 301
WRITE—pen, pencil; any writing instrument, 93, 185, 186, 187

x-ray, 129

YEAR, 317
YELLOW, 273
Yes/No Questions, 44
YESTERDAY, 21, 30, 146, 148
yet (BUT), 91, 230
YOU, 14, 15, 20, 35, 37, 38, 44, 47, 48, 52, 53, 66, 69, 71, 92, 96, 97, 98, 102, 115, 117, 118, 129, 130, 132, 146, 152, 153, 155, 161, 171, 182, 187, 193, 220, 245, 256, 261, 275, 281, 287, 289, 290, 292, 293, 297, 333
YOU AND I, 193
YOUR, 21, 63, 147, 154
YOURSELF—This sign may also be used idiomatically in the same way as "Aloha" and "Shalom" are used, that is, to say "Hello," "Goodbye," and to wish someone the best of everything. 64

ZERO, 152, 302